Sacraments of Life
Life of the Sacraments

Leonardo Boff

Translated by John Drury

Pastoral Press
Portland, Oregon

Translated from the Portuguese
Os Sacramentos da Vida e a Vida dos Sacramentos
Editora Vozes Ltda
Petrópolis, Brazil
1975

A Division of OCP
5536 N.E. Hassalo
Portland, OR 97213
Phone: 1-800-LITURGY (548-8749)
Email: liturgy@ocp.org
Web site: http//www.ocp.org
Printed in the United Sates of America.

ISBN: 0-912405-38-4

TS:1022

Contents

I dedicate this little book to the mountain
that ever visits my window.
Sometimes the sun sears it. Sometimes the sun caresses it.
Often the rain scourges it.
Now and then the snow gently envelops it.
I have never heard the mountain complain about
the heat or the cold.
It has never charged anything for its majestic beauty.
It has never even asked for thanks.
It simply gives of itself free of charge.
It is no less majestic when the sun caresses it
than when the wind lashes it.
It does not care or get upset if people
scrutinize it or climb it.
The mountain is like God.
It supports everything, endures everything,
welcomes and shelters everything.
God behaves in the same way.
That is why the mountain is a sacrament of God,
revealing, reminding, pointing to, sending us
back to.
Because the mountain is like that
I gratefully dedicate this book to it.
This book attempts to speak the sacramental language
that the mountain does not speak but—far more important—is.

1

Gateway to the Sacramental Structure

This little book will be meaningful only to those minds and hearts that live in our world of science and technology but are of a different spirit. This different spirit permits them to see beyond any immediate landscape and to travel beyond any given horizon. Today that spirit dwells in the underground depths of our cultural experience. It is like an underground stream feeding our wells and springs, which in turn feed the surface waters. We do not see it but it is the most important thing, because it humanizes things and our relationships with them. It detects the secret meaning inscribed in them.

Humans are not simply beings who manipulate their world. They are capable of reading the message that the world carries within it, that is written in all the things making up the world. Both ancient and modern semiologists have seen quite clearly that things, besides being things, form a system of signs. They are so many syllables of a great alphabet, an alphabet in the service of a message inscribed in things. The message can be described and deciphered by anyone with open eyes.

Humans are beings capable of reading the world's message. They are never illiterate with respect to this particular alphabet. They can read and interpret the message in a multiplicity of languages. To live is to read and interpret. In the ephemeral, they can read the Permanent; in the temporal, the Eternal; in the world, God. Then the ephemeral is transfigured into a sign of the presence of the Permanent, the temporal into a symbol of the reality of the Eternal, the world into a great and grand sacrament of God. The sacramental structure emerges when things begin to speak and human beings begin to hear their voices. On the frontispiece of this structure is inscribed the phrase: all of reality is but a sign. A sign of what? Of another reality, a Reality that founds and grounds all things: God.

I don't think modern humanity has lost its sense of the symbolic and the sacramental. Today's human beings are just as much human beings as those of other cultural settings and historical ages. They, too, produce symbols which express their inner life and they, too, are capable of deciphering the symbolic meaning of the world. They may well have become blind and deaf to symbols and sacramental rites that are now stiff and anachronistic; but that is the fault of the rites themselves, not of modern human beings. We cannot hide the fact that in the Christian sacramental universe there has been a process of ritual mummification. The present-day rites hardly speak for themselves. They have to be explained. And a sign that has to be explained is no sign at all. What should be explained, after all, is not the sign but the Mystery contained in the sign. Because of this ritual mummification, secularized modern human beings are suspicious of the Christian sacramental universe. They may well feel tempted to break all ties with religious symbolism. But if they actually do that, they do not simply make a break with an important religious treasure; they also close the window of their own soul, because the symbolic and the sacramental are profound dimensions imbedded in human reality.

Sacraments as an Interplay between Human Beings, the World, and God

Phenomenologists and anthropologists have described in detail the interplay between human beings and the world. It takes place on three successive levels. At the first level human beings experience *awe and wonder*. Things evoke both admiration and fear. Human beings examine them from every angle, gradually replacing surprise with certainty. The second level is the end-point of that process: *domestication*. Human beings manage to interpret the things that caused awe and wonder, thus gaining dominion over them. Science is situated on this level. It fits phenomena into a coherent system in order to tame or domesticate them. Finally, at the third level, humans become *habituated* to objects. They are now a part of the human landscape.

This interplay changes both human beings and the objects as it takes place. The latter are no longer mere objects. They have become signs and symbols of encounter, effort, conquest, and the inner life of the human being. Domesticated objects begin to speak, to tell the story of their interplay with humanity. They are transformed into sacraments. The human world, even if it be material and technical, is never merely material and technical. It is symbolic and fraught with meaning. This is perfectly well-known by those who direct the masses through the communications media. Human beings are guided not so much by ideologies as by symbols and myths that are activated through the collective unconscious. A TV commercial presents a certain product. Those who use this brand partake of "the divine" and share the life of the gods: handsome, rich people in their beautiful mansions, surrounded by their glamorous lovers and enjoying the ecstasy of love, all conflicts and problems solved. The whole staging is ritual and symbolic. These profane and profaning sacraments are designed to evoke participation in a dreamy, perfect reality, to give people the feeling that they have already transcended this world of conflicts and difficulties.

Human beings possess this extraordinary capability. They can turn an object into a symbol and an action into a rite. Let me give you a Brazilian example. When someone comes to visit us in southern Brazil, we immediately offer that person a

3

gourd of hot, unsweetened tea or coffee. We sit down and relax in the open air. We drink from the same gourd and suck up the beverage through the same siphon. But we do not drink this beverage because we are thirsty, because we have a taste for bitter things, or because the beverage "does wonders" and will get rid of all traces of indigestion. Our action has a different meaning. It is a ritual action in which we celebrate our meeting and savor our friendship. The center of attention is not the beverage but the person. The beverage serves a sacramental function.

The difference was brought out clearly by Paul, who had a complaint against the Corinthians (1 Cor 11:20-22). Some Corinthians were coming to the eucharistic banquet only to satisfy their hunger and quench their thirst. Such people had lost the point and meaning of a sacrament. We hold the eucharistic banquet, not to satisfy our hunger, but to celebrate and render present the Lord's Supper. The act of eating to satisfy our hunger and the act of celebrating the Last Supper may be the same; but the meaning of the act is different in each case. At the eucharistic banquet the ordinary daily act of eating signifies something different. It has a different, symbolic meaning. That makes it a sacrament.

Sacraments, then, are deeply rooted in human life. To cut that tie would be to cut the root of life itself and ruin the interplay between human beings and the world.

Christianity sees itself, not primarily as an architectonic system of saving truths, but rather as the communication of divine life within this world. The world, things, and human beings have come to be penetrated by the generous sap of God. Things are bearers of salvation and a Mystery. That is why they are sacramental. To a large extent, Christian opposition to Marxism is due to its different understanding of matter. Christianity says that matter is not merely an object for human manipulation and possession. It is a bearer of God and a place where we encounter salvation. Matter is sacramental.

4

This universal sacramentality reached its maximum concentration in Jesus Christ, the primordial Sacrament of God. With his ascension into heaven and disappearance from human view, Christ's sacramental density passed to the church, which is the Sacrament of Christ prolonged through the ages. The universal sacrament of the church takes concrete shape in various situations of life, grounding the sacramental structure that is mainly centered in the seven sacraments.

It should be pointed out, however, that the seven sacraments do not swallow up all the sacramental richness of the church. Everything the church does has a sacramental density because the church is fundamentally a sacrament. Neither is grace tied down to the seven major signs of the faith. It comes to us in other sacramental signs, for example, a word from a friend, an article in the newspaper, a message lost in space, a look of entreaty, an act of reconciliation, or a challenge posed by poverty and oppression. Anything can be a sacramental vehicle of divine grace. The ability to detect and then welcome salvation under such concrete signs is the mark and task of mature faith. Today's Christians must be educated to see sacraments above and beyond the confines of the seven sacraments. As adults, they should know how to enact rites that signify and celebrate the breakthrough of grace into their lives and communities. One of the purposes of this essay is to further that process.

History and Story as the Language of the Sacraments

Since sacraments, whether profane or sacred, arise out of a human interaction with the world and God, the structure of their language is narrative rather than argumentative. They do not argue or try to persuade. They aim to narrate and celebrate the story of human encounters with the objects, situations, and other humans that provoked them to transcend their immediate position, evoked and made present a higher reality, and convoked their sacramental encounter with God.

For centuries theology was argumentative. It sought to speak to the minds of human beings and convince them of the truth of religion. Its success was meager. Usually it was convincing only to those already convinced. Theology elaborated its themes under the illusion that God, his saving plan, the future promised to humanity, and the mystery of Jesus Christ as God and human being could be accepted intellectually before people had accepted them in their real lives and undergone a transformation of their hearts. Forgotten, at least in manuals of theology and apologetics, was the fact that religious truth is never an abstract formula or the end-product of logical reasoning. It is basically and primarily a vital experience, an encounter with ultimate meaning. Only then comes the cultural articulation and linkup, which translates it into formulas and explicitates its inherent rational element.

As we shall see in the course of our reflection in this volume, sacraments take shape essentially in an encounter process. Underlying them always is a story that begins: "There was once a mug . . . a piece of bread . . . a cigarette butt . . . a Jesus who was both God and human being . . . a supper Jesus celebrated . . . and act of pardon Jesus performed." Thus, as the semiologists of theological discourse tell us, the language of religion and sacrament is never merely descriptive. In fact, it is mainly *evocative*. It narrates an event, relates a miracle, or describes a revelatory divine breakthrough in order to evoke in human beings God's reality, behavior, and promise of salvation. That is the first and primary point of interest.

Let me give a personal example here. I am standing in front of a mountain. I can describe the mountain, its history over billions of years, and its physiochemical composition. In so doing, I am being a scientist. But beyond these real dimensions there is another dimension. In me the mountain evokes or calls up images of grandeur, majesty, stateliness, solidity, and eternity. It calls to my mind God, who has often been called Rock. Here rock serves as a symbol for solidity, stateliness, majesty, and grandeur. It evokes those features and serves as a sacrament of them. Religious language operates mainly in the same horizon, in the realm of evocation. Sacraments are essentially evocations of a past and a future that are lived in the present.

Religious language is sacramental and *self-involving*. Since it is not just descriptive but mainly evocative, it always involves a person with things. No one is left neutral. It touches human beings deep inside themselves, setting up an encounter that changes human beings and the world. In *The House of the Dead* Dostoyevsky tells us about his release from prison. As he leaves it, he contemplates the irons that had been on his legs. They had been hammered off on the anvil, and he sees the pieces on the floor. Those pieces on the floor enable him to savor freedom. Before leaving the prison, he makes a farewell visit to the palisades and dirty cells. They have become familiar and fraternal because he has spent a bit of his life with them and now they are part of his life. He feels involvement with all those things because they are no longer merely things. They have become sacraments, evoking his suffering, long vigils, and yearning for liberation.

Finally, religious and sacramental language is *performance-oriented*. It tends to alter human praxis, to induce conversion. It summons people to open up and accept something that will become part of their actual way of living.

This essay attempts to spell out the language of story and narrative insofar as it is evocative, self-involving, and performance-oriented with respect to the sacramental realm. My aim is to recapture the religious richness contained in the symbolic and sacramental universe that inhabits our daily life. The sacraments are not the private property of the sacred hierarchy. They are basic constituents of human life. Faith sees grace present in the most elementary acts of life. So it ritualizes them and elevates them to the sacramental level.

I should like to awaken readers to the sacramental dimension that lies dormant or profanized in our lives. Once awakened again, we shall be able to celebrate the mysterious but concrete presence of grace in our world. God was always there, even before we may have been awake to the fact. Now that we are awake, we can see that the world is a sacrament of God. People who manage to perceive and appreciate the sacraments of life are very close to, or rather already immersed in, the life of the sacraments.

2

Our Family Mug as Sacrament

There is this aluminum mug of ours, the good old kind that is bright and shiny. The handle is broken, but that gives it the air of an antique. The family's eleven children of all ages drank from it. It has accompanied the family on its many moves: from rural countryside to town, from town to city, from city to metropolis. There were births and deaths. It has shared everything. It has always been there. It is the ongoing mystery of life and its continuity amid differing situations of life and mortal existence. The mug endures, old but still shiny. I think it must have been old even when it first came into the house. But its elderliness is really youthfulness because it generates and bestows life. It is the centerpiece of our kitchen.

When I drink from it, I do not drink just water. I drink in freshness, gentleness, familiarity, my family history, and the memory of a greedy little boy quenching his thirst. Whatever sort of water it may be, in that mug it is always good and fresh. Everyone in our home takes a drink from it when he or she wants to quench a thirst. As if it were a ritual, we all exclaim: How good it is to drink from this mug! How good the water is here! From the newspapers we gather that the water is ill-treated. It comes from the polluted city river and it is full of chlorine; but, thanks to our mug, it becomes good, healthy, fresh, and sweet.

The boy leaves home, travels to other parts of the world, and engages in various studies. Then he returns home. He kisses his mother, hugs his brothers and sisters. The bouts of loneliness

9

he has suffered at various times are overcome. Words are few, but the looks are long and careful. We must drink in other people before we can love them. Eyes that drink in people speak the language of the heart. Only then does the mouth voice its superficialities: You look so fine and handsome! How grownup you have become! The eye and its look say nothing of the sort. Its glance speaks the ineffable language of love. Only the light of heart and mind understands. "Mama, I'm thirsty! I want a drink from our old mug!"

Her child has drunk from many waters: the waters of San Pellegrino, Germany, England, and France; the fine water of Greece, the sparkling fountain waters of the Alps, the Tirol, and Rome; the waters of San Francisco, Ouro Fino, Teresópolis, and Petrópolis. So many different waters, but none of them like this water. He downs a mug of water, but not to slake his bodily thirst. Many waters can do that. He downs this mug of water to slake his thirst for the family archetype, the household gods of his parents, brothers, and sisters. His is an archeological thirst for the roots from which the sap of life comes. Only the family mug can slake that particular thirst. He drinks his first mugful of water greedily, ending with a long sigh as a diving swimmer might upon resurfacing. Then he drinks another mugful of water slowly: to taste the mystery that the mug contains and signifies.

Why is the water in the mug good and sweet, fresh and healthy? Because the mug itself is a sacrament. The mug-sacrament gives the water its goodness, sweetness, freshness, and healthiness.

Today many people no longer know what a sacrament is. The people of old did know. It cost me a great deal to learn. For five years I spent many hours every day reading and studying what has been written about the sacraments. To put it in terms of Christian chronology, I ranged from biblical times to the present day. It was a battle of mind and spirit. One result was 552 pages that were printed and published as a book.

But that was not really the main result. After all that effort, rage, joy, cursing, and blessing, I discovered what was always there for people to discover. I verified what was blatant and obvious. Sacraments were always alive and well, and everyone lives them. But the sacraments themselves were not aware of that, and few people knew it. I turned and looked again at the landscape that is always right in front of one's nose. Daily life is full of sacraments. In the archeology of everyday life the sacraments thrive. They are alive, and true, and experienced in everyone's life. My chunk of mountain, my family's mug, and all the other things I shall mention in this book ceased to be mere things for me. They became people and they now speak. We can hear their voice and their message. They have an inside, a heart. They have become sacraments. In other words, they are signs that contain, exhibit, recall, visualize, and communicate another reality, a reality different from themselves but present in them.

The modern world lives in the midst of sacraments but does not have the open eye to visualize them reflectively. The reason is that it sees things only as things. It views them only from the outside. When we look inside them, we perceive that they have a crack through which a higher light enters. The light illuminates things, making them clear and transparent. Let us take another look at the family mug in this perspective.

The Outside, Scientific View of Our Family Mug

Our family mug can be viewed from the outside. It is just like any other mug, but perhaps uglier, older, and less serviceable. It is made of aluminum. It would interest physicists insofar as they analyze the physical components of aluminum. Economists might offer points of information about the extraction, production, commercialization, and pricing of aluminum. If it

11

were a mug from the time of Augustan Rome, historians might be interested in pinpointing its place in time and space. Artists might consider it an object without any esthetic value, and museums would not seek it out as something significant. All the practitioners of these disciplines would view our mug merely as a thing.

It is typical of us moderns, particularly from the fifteenth century on, to view everything as a thing we can pore over and analyze in order to determine what we can see in it. We tend to turn everything into an object of study and science: God, the human being, history, and nature. We set them in front of us and fix our scrutiny on them. We can indulge in many sciences with respect to one and the same object because it may be of interest from different scientific viewpoints. That is why it is said that today we know more and more about less and less.

Analyzed thus, our family mug is just another object among many others. It has not had a history with anyone or entered anyone's life.

The Inside, Sacramental View of Our Family Mug

It may be that someone has captivated a mug. The mug saved someone from the burning thirst of an endless desert. Or, as in my own personal case, the mug became part of the story of my personal and family life. It is unique. There is no other mug like it. It has ceased to be an object because it has become a subject. Like any subject, it has a history that can be told and remembered. We have had a profound relationship with this thing, the mug, and that loving relationship has given us an outlook whereby we see inestimable value in the mug. It is now inscribed in the human realm and begins to speak. It tells of childhood and the thirsts satisfied by it. It tells of the water we used to seek a good six hundred meters from our house in a deep well of pure water. That quest caused us to utter cries of profanity and pain on wintry mornings or rainy afternoons, but it also made the water more precious and pure.

The mug tells the history of our family, which it has accompanied in life and in death. Increasingly it became part of the family. In the end it became a child, the one surrounded by the most affection. Today it is still there to speak to us and remind us, faithfully and humbly serving water that it has made sweet, fresh, and good. This is the inside view of our family mug. Our relationship with it has turned it into a family sacrament.

Looking at a thing from the outside, I bend over it, scrutinize it, manipulate it, transform it, and allow it to be nothing more than a thing, an object of human use and abuse. That is the scientific way of thinking that characterizes our modern age. It is not bad; it is simply different. How could we be hostile to our own world and its scientific outlook, when that outlook makes life easier and longer, expands the activity of our arms and legs and eyes with amazing instruments, and thus increasingly makes us masters of nature?

But is the human being only that: a robot in action, a computer for data and information, a microsopic and macroscopic lens on the world? Or is the human being someone who can have a human relationship with things, see values, and detect a meaning in them?

When I look inside a thing, I don't concentrate on the thing itself but on the value and meaningfulness it has for me. It ceases to be a mere thing and becomes a symbol and sign for evoking, provoking, and convoking situations, reminiscences, and the meaning it incarnates and expresses. Sacrament signifies precisely that real aspect of the world. Without ceasing to be world, it speaks to us of another world: the human world of deeply felt experiences, unquestionable values, and the meaning that gives life richness and fullness. To grasp this way of thinking is to open oneself to the possibility of accepting and

13

welcoming the sacraments of faith, which radicalize the natural sacraments we experience in our daily lives.

Sacraments change the world. Water might be any water. But when it is served and savored in a mug become sacrament, the water becomes good, sweet, fresh, and healthful for those who grasp and live the inside view of things. It communicates and shares life, telling of the mystery that dwells in things.

Our aluminum mug is there in the kitchen, dwelling in tranquil dignity among other household objects and things. It is old, but only it preserves the perennial youthfulness of life. For only it is alive amid dead things. Only it is a subject amid so many mere objects. Only it speaks amid so many mute things. Only it is a sacrament in the humble surroundings of a family kitchen.

3

My Father's Cigarette Butt as Sacrament

There is a little treasure buried back in a drawer. It is a little flask with a cigarette butt in it. This little butt is made of straw and the yellowish tobacco people are wont to smoke in southern Brazil. Nothing new about all that. But this insignificant cigarette butt has a unique history. It speaks to my heart and evokes endless nostalgia and longing.

On August 11, 1965, I was in Munich, West Germany. I remember the day well. Outside, the houses were welcoming the strong sun of a European summer. Multicolored flowers were blossoming in the parks or fluttering gaily from windows. It was 2:00 P.M. The mailman brought me my first letter from home. It was fraught with the nostalgia of the journey it had made. I opened it hastily. Everyone at home had written. It almost seemed to be a newspaper or journal. It had an air of mystery.

You should already be in Munich when you read these lines. Though different from all the other letters, this letter, too, brings you a beautiful message. Seen from the standpoint of faith, the news it brings you is truly good news. A few days ago, God asked a tribute of love, faith, and serious thanksgiving from us. He came down into the midst of our family, looked around at each one of us, and chose for himself the most perfect and most mature one of us, the holiest and the best: our beloved papa. Dear Leonardo, God did not take him away from us; he left him

15

with us even more. He did not snatch papa away from the joy of our holidays; he planted him even more deeply in the memory of us all. God did not steal papa away from our presence; he left him even more present with us. He did not take him; he left him with us. Papa did not go away; he came to us. Papa did not go; he came so that he would be papa even more, so that papa would be present now and always with all of us here in Brazil, with you in West Germany, with Ruy and Clodovis in Louvain, and with Waldemar in the United States.

The letter continued with the testimony of each child. The death that had taken up its place in the living heart of a fifty-four year old man was celebrated as a sister, as a communion feast uniting a family dispersed in three different countries. A profound serenity bubbled up amid the turbulent tears.

Faith illuminates and exorcises the absurdity of death. Death is the true birthday *(dies natalis)* of the human being. And so, in the catacombs of the old monastery, in the presence of so many living figures from the past—from William of Ockham to the humble infirmarian who had just been born to God a few days ago, on three successive days I celebrated the holy Mass of Christmas for the man who, far away in his true homeland, was already celebrating his final and definitive birthday. How the ancient texts took on a strange profundity: *"puer natus est nobis . . ."*

The next day, in the envelope that had brought me the news of a death, I noticed a sign of the life of the man who had given life to us in every sense of the word. It was a yellowed cigarette butt, the last he had smoked moments before coronary thrombosis liberated him once and for all from this weary existence. The deeply feminine and sacramental intuition of a sister had prompted her to include the cigarette butt in the envelope.

From that point on, the cigarette butt ceased to be a cigarette butt. It became a sacrament and remained one. It is alive and speaks of life. It accompanies life. Its typical color, its strong smell, and its burnt end mean it is still lit in my life. So it is of inestimable value. It belongs to the heart of life and the life of the heart. It recalls and renders present the figure of papa who, with the passage of years, had already become a family archetype and a touchstone for the fundamental values of all his children. "From his lips we have heard, from his life we have learned: one who does not live to serve is of no use for living." That is the epitaph we placed on his tombstone.

The Sacramental Function

Whenever a reality of this world, without leaving the world, evokes another, different reality, it takes on a sacramental function. It ceases to be a thing and becomes a sign or symbol. Every sign is a sign *of* some thing or some value *for* someone. As a thing, it may be absolutely irrelevant. As a sign, it can take on precious and priceless value. Thus, as a thing, the straw cigarette gets thrown into the garbage; but as a symbol, it is preserved as a priceless treasure.

What makes something a sacrament? As we have already seen in describing my family mug as a sacrament, it is the inner human view of things that transmutes them into sacraments. It is living familiarly and intimately with things that creates and re-creates them symbolically. It is the time we spend with them, the taming of them, the insertion of them into our own experience that humanizes them and makes them speak the language of human beings. Sacraments reveal a way of thinking that is typically human. There is a real sacramental way of thinking, just as there is a scientific way of thinking. At the first stage of sacramental thinking, everything is seen *sub specie humanitatis.*

Everything reveals the human being: its successful or unsuccessful experiences, that is, its encounter with the manifold manifestations of the world. In this encounter human beings do not approach the world from a neutral standpoint. They form judgments, discover values, make interpretations. Familiarity

17

with the world means that human beings create their own habitations, which is the little parcel of the domesticated world in which each thing has its own name and place. There things are not simply made sport of. They share in the human order, become familiar things, reveal what the human being is and how it is that. They speak of the inhabitant and draw his or her portrait.

The more deeply human beings relate to the world and to the things of *their own* world, the more clearly sacramentality shows up. Then there emerge the native homeland that is more than the geographical boundaries of a country, the place of our birth that is more than a parcel of government land, the native city that is more than the sum of its houses and inhabitants, the parental home that is more than a stone building. In all those things dwell values, good and evil spirits, and the lineaments of a human landscape. Sacramental thinking means that the roads we travel, the mountains we see, the rivers that bathe our lands, the houses that inhabit our neighborhoods, and the persons that create our society, are not simply people, houses, rivers, mountains, and roads like all the others in the world. They are unique and incomparable. They are a part of ourselves. So we rejoice and suffer over their fate. We lament the felling of the huge tree in our town square or the demolition of an old shed. Something of ourselves dies along with them. Why? Because they are no longer merely things. They are sacraments in our life, be it blessed or cursed.

The Sacramental Dimensions of Life

Everything is, or can become, a sacrament. It depends on human beings and the way they look at things. The world will reveal its sacramental nature insofar as human beings look at it humanely, relating to it and letting the world come inside them to become *their* world.

The classical authors tell us that human beings are, in some way, all things. If that is true, then it is also true that all things can become sacraments for them, so long as human beings open up to all things and welcome them into their human abode. Isn't that the essential vocation of human beings with respect to the world? To humanize it? To make it their dwelling and draw it out of its opacity? And isn't the sacramental way of looking at things the way to go about that vocation? Then the whole world, not just some little parcel of it, would be their friendly and familiar homeland inhabited by fraternity and a tranquility of order reigning over all things.

Who would have said that a cigarette butt could become a sacrament? But there it is in the back of my drawer. Now and then I open the flask. An aroma escapes. The color and texture of a living past take shape. The drawer does not contain the grandeur of the presence created. The mind's eye sees my father alive, rendered present in the cigarette butt: cutting the straw, parceling out the tobacco, igniting the lighter, taking long drags of his cigarette, giving lessons, reading the newspaper, burning his shirts with the sparks, plunging into arduous office work at night, smoking . . . smoking. His last cigarette went out with his own mortal life. But something continues to remain lit, because of the sacrament.

4

Homemade Bread as Sacrament

Now and then at home mama makes bread. The fact never ceases to be curious and amazing. In a big-city apartment, with plenty of bakeries all around, someone indulges in the luxury or toil of making bread! It is not a matter of dire physical need. The bread is not desperately needed to satisfy hunger. Bread-making is in the tradition of an ancient rite, stemming from a need that is far more basic than the need to satisfy one's hunger. It is the repetition of an archetypal gesture. Primitive humans repeated certain acts, primordial acts that made them feel one with the beginning of things and the hidden meaning of the cosmos. So it is in this case. Breadmaking is the repetition of an act that is rich in human meaningfulness and goes far beyond any problem of immediate need.

Nowdays the bread is baked in the narrow confines of a gas oven, not in the huge brick kiln as it once was. The bread is kneaded slowly by hand. It takes effort and pain to knead things. Once baked, it was be shared out among my brothers and sisters, who now have families of their own and live else-where. They all find it delicious: "Mama's bread." It has a special quality that is not to be found in the anonymous bread, without any history, that can be bought at the neighborhood bakery or downtown supermarket

What is the special quality in this particular bread? Why is this bread shared out among family members? Because this bread is sacramental bread. It is made of flour and the other in-gredients found in any loaf of bread, and yet it is different because it evokes another human reality. That other human reality is rendered present in and with the bread made by my mother. She is now an old widow with white hair, but she is also more closely rooted to the original gestures of life, hence to the deeper meaning that family things embody.

Her bread evokes remembrance of a past when bread was made weekly with much sacrifice. Eleven little mouths, like so many baby birds, would wait expectantly for food from their mother. She got up very early, she who became our symbol of the valiant woman *(mulier fortis)* and great mother *(magna mater)*. She heaped up plenty of flour, immaculately white. She added yeast and many eggs. Sometimes she also included sweet potatoes. Then, with her strong arms and hands, she kneaded the mixture until it formed a homogeneous mass. This was topped with a little maize flour of a thicker sort, and the whole concoction was covered with a large white towel.

When we got up, the huge mass was already on the kitchen table. We little ones peeked under the towel to see the smooth, spongy mass. With our index fingers we secretly gave it a little poke. Now it was time to light the oven. Much firewood was needed. Who was to go out to look for wood today? Everyone was delighted, however, when the bread came out of the oven in rosy-colored health.

As in a ritual, everyone got a piece. The bread was never cut up. Even today it is broken into pieces by hand, perhaps in remembrance of him who was recognized in the breaking of the bread (Lk 24:30-35).

That bread of ours—massed with hard work, leavened and cooked in expectation, and eaten with delight—is a basic symbol of life. Whenever papa was traveling, mama had a batch of bread waiting for him on his return. Like us children, he reveled in the freshly made bread, which he ate with Italian cheese or salami and a good glass of wine. No one more than he savored the joy of plain living in the generous frugality of such primordial human meals.

When bread is made in that old apartment today and distributed to my brothers and sisters, the act is a remembrance of those bygone days. None of us children know this in a conscious way. The knowledge is buried in our unconscious and in the deep structures of our lives. The baked homemade bread brings to our conscious memory what lies buried in the depths of the family unconscious. That can always be called up and relived. We children will always find that mama's bread is the best in the whole world: not because it is the product of some secret formula that brings wealth to merchants but because it is an archetypal, sacramental bread. As a sacrament, it is part of our lives as brothers and sisters. It is good for our hearts and nourishes our lives. It is saturated with a meaningfulness that is transparent in the material reality of the bread.

Sacramental Thinking: A Total Experience

We have already given a little consideration to sacramental thinking. It is marked by a specific human way of approaching things. Instead of approaching things with indifference, in this case human beings create ties with things and allow them to become a real part of their lives. From the moment we captivate and tame something, it begins to be a part of our world. It becomes unique. Remember what the little prince says in Saint-Exupéry's work *(The Little Prince)*. Comparing the numerous roses around him to the single, unique rose of his own planet B-612, he tells the roses:

"You are not at all like my rose," he said. "As yet you are nothing. No one has captivated or tamed you, and you have not captivated or tamed anyone. You are like my fox once was. He was merely a fox like a hundred thousand other foxes. But I made him my friend, and now he is unique in all the world."

The boy's rose and fox had been transformed into sacraments. They now made visible the sharing of life, the work of creating ties, and the reality of hope and time lost. Wheat is of no use to the fox, but the little prince has golden hair. So the golden wheat in the fields begins to speak to the fox. It becomes a sacrament, reminding him of the little prince. So the fox begins to love the noise of the wind as it sweeps over the golden wheat field.

So it is with our homemade bread. It is unique amid all the bread in the world. Only that bread reminds us of another time in our lives because of its aroma, its unmistakable flavor, and the hard work of our mother than went into it. But how does the bread exactly recall that to our minds?

Immanence—Transcendence—Transparence

Our bread recalls to our minds something that is not bread, something that *transcends* the bread itself. The bread itself is *immanent*. It is right here with its weight and its component elements: flour, eggs, water, salt, and leaven. It is opaque. But this immanent reality, the bread, renders present a transcendent reality that is not bread. How does this take place? In and through the bread. The bread then becomes *transparent*, revealing a transcendent reality. It ceases to be merely immanent. It is no longer like any other bread. Now it is different because it calls up and makes present, in and through itself (immanence and transparence), something that goes beyond itself (transcendence).

The bread becomes transparent and diaphanous, revealing such realities as food, hunger, mama's sweat and effort, our joy in sharing bread with each other, and papa's homecoming. Suddenly the whole world of childhood is there again, made present in and through the reality of bread.

A sacrament embodies a total experience. No longer is the world divided between immanence and transcendence. There

24

is another intermediary category, transparence, that embraces both immanence and transcendence. The latter two realities are not opposed to one another or mutually exclusive. They meet and communicate with each other. Here "transparence" means that the transcendent is rendered present in the immanent so that the latter makes the reality of the former transparent. The transcendent breaks through into the immanent, transfigures it, and thus makes it transparent.

If we understand that, then we understand the structure of a sacrament and the nature of sacramental thinking. If we do not understand that, we simply know nothing about the realm of symbols and sacraments.

Thus, the transparent sacrament participates in both the transcendent world and the immanent world. That entails tensions and temptations, of course. A sacrament might tend to become wholly immanent and exclude the transcendent. Then it would be opaque, lacking the brilliant radiance of transcendence that transfigures the dull weight of matter. Or a sacrament might become wholly transcendental and exclude the immanent. Then it would be abstract, losing the tangible concreteness that immanence confers on transcendence. In either case the transparence of things is lost and the sacrament is perverted.

Now and then at home we eat the shared bread made by mama. It is good for us as papa's homecoming used to be. It is much more than food. It is the fruit of sorrow and joy, of brotherly and sisterly love, of surprise homecomings, of toilsome quests for firewood, of hunger satisfied. It is good for the heart. It nourishes the spirit more than the body because it is a sacrament.

25

5

A Christmas Candle as Sacrament

Snow was falling ever so lightly but steadily. It had already covered the fields with a thick white mantle. All you could see around was a blanket of snow and the murky shadows of cypresses startling the eye. For me, a person from the tropics, it never ceased to be an amazing spectacle.

It was Christmas Eve, my first Christmas outside my native country. I felt a mixture of melancholy and nostalgia on the one hand, expectation and inner peace on the other. All my feelings were only heightened by the atmosphere of a cold European winter with a temperature of 22° centigrade below zero. I was in Berchtesgaden, a little town in southeastern Bavaria only slightly tainted by the name of Adolf Hitler, who had built his *D-Haus* retreat here but never really came to use it.

The Franciscan monastery in the center of the town was almost lost amid the dazzle of snow and the opaque curtain of sky. Only its steeple punctured the sky and its curtain of snow. I spent the afternoon meandering with a walking stick through the decorated streets. The local custom was to have lighted lanterns in the windows, signals that the baby child was coming. He would come only once; one had to be ready for him.

Late that afternoon I heard many confessions. Most of the penitents were French people, who were beginning to indulge in the winter sports provided by the surrounding mountains. Everybody obviously wanted to prepare for Christmas. We priests were helping other people to prepare for Christmas, but we had no time for our own preparation. We were not doing a good job of celebrating Christmas, but we were being of service to those who wanted to celebrate it. At the 6:00 P.M. Mass, while everybody else was heading for the babe in the manger and remembering his story, we priests were listening to other stories of other loves in the confessionals. If only on this one day, I thought to myself, we could all pay heed to one and the same story of history: the historical story of God's love for and in the world, of his nearness to us, of his great and awesome glory reduced to the size of a baby but infinitely magnified in beneficence.

Around 11:00 P.M. we heard the loud noise of crunching footsteps. From every direction the peasants were descending the mountains for Midnight Mass, their light illuminating the snow and making it look like blue sky. It was their simple, straightforward way of showing their affection for the smiling babe nestled between oxen and donkeys. Midnight Mass was beautiful. The peasants sang, dressed in leather britches to the knee, long stockings, and big boots. They played the typical folk melodies of Bavaria on their instruments. They looked like the shepherds of Bethlehem and could well have been they. When it was all over, a profound silence came over the scene. We could see their lights as they hurried home over the hillsides, praising and glorifying God for all they had seen and heard.

Alone once more in my room, I reverently opened the parcel as I envisioned images of Christmas back home. The scene was much the same as here in Bavaria, but without snow. Inside the parcel was a big candle: dark red, elaborately wrought, with a huge metal stand. A light now illuminated my lonely night and long shadows flickered along the wall. I no longer felt alone. Far away from home I had experienced the miracle of every Christmas: the joyous feast of brotherhood and sisterhood for all human beings. Someone had understood the newborn babe's message, had made a foreigner a neighbor, a stranger a brother.

Today, many years later, that Christmas candle still keeps Christmas vigil on my bookcase. Once a year, on that blessed night, I light it. I shall continue to do so. Its light reminds me of a happy night when I had felt lonely amid the snow of Bavaria. It reminds me of an act of giving that was more than a mere gesture of the hand. It brings back to mind the giving of a gift that was more than mere giving. It re-presents Christmas with all its human and divine significance. My Christmas candle is more than any other Christmas candle, however artistic the latter may be. For it is a sacrament of Christmas.

Everything a Sacrament from God's Standpoint

So far we have been considering human sacraments. Now it is time for us to begin looking at divine sacraments. Viewed *sub specie humanitatis,* all things express and symbolize humanity. They are human sacraments. The more we allow things to enter our lives, the more they manifest their sacramental nature, that is, become meaningful and unique for us. They evoke the experiences we have actually lived with them.

So it was with my Christmas candle. That Christmas passed and my experience of it was overlaid with others. But the candle remains, ensuring that the past will not remain simply the past. The candle reminds and evokes. A sacrament redeems us from the past and brings the dead fact to life. Thanks to it, my Christmas in Berchtesgaden ever remains a presence. And there are human sacraments that inhabit the life of each human being.

There are also divine sacraments. Human beings possess a profound experience of God. God is not a concept learned from the catechism. God is not the apex of the pyramid that neatly completes our system of thought. God is an inner experience that touches the very roots of our existence. Without God everything would be absurd. We would not comprehend ourselves, much less the world. God surfaces for us as a mystery, so absolute and radical a mystery that it has its annunciation in everything, penetrates everything, shines through everything.

If God is the unique Absolute, then everything in existence is a revelation of God. For those who experience God as alive in this way, the immanent world becomes transparent, allowing this divine, transcendent reality to shine through it. The world becomes diaphonous. As St. Irenaeus put it: "Nothing is a vacuum in the face of God. Everything is a sign of God" (*Adv. Haer.*, 4:21). Everything speaks of God, of God's beauty, goodness, and mystery. A mountain is no longer just a mountain; it is in the service of the divine grandeur it incarnates and evokes. The sun is more than just the sun; it is the sacrament of the divine light that illuminates everything, from garbage heap to majestic cathedral, from beggar to pope. Human beings are no longer merely human beings. They are the great sacrament of God and God's intelligence, love, and mysteriousness. Jesus of Nazareth is more than just a human being from Galilee. He is the Christ, the living sacrament of God incarnated in him. The church is more than the society of the baptized; it is the sacrament of the resurrected Christ making himself present in history.

For those who see everything in terms of God, the entire world is one grand sacrament. Every thing and every historical event appear as sacraments of God and God's divine will. But that is only possible for those who see God as alive. For those who do not, the world is opaque and merely immanent. Insofar as people allow themselves, by toil and effort, to be taken and penetrated by God, they are rewarded with the divine transparence of all things.

The mystics offer us the best proof of this. St. Francis of Assisi immersed himself so deeply in the mystery of God that suddenly he found everything transfigured. Everything spoke to him of God and Christ: the worms along the wayside; the lambs in the fields; the birds in the trees; fire, and death, which

30

he came to call sister death. God comes to fill everything: immanence, transparence, and transcendence. As St. Paul put it: "There is only one God and Father of all, who is over all **transcendence,** works through all **transparence,** and is in all **immanence**" (Eph 4:6). With Pierre Teilhard de Chardin, who lived the same sort of sacramental wisdom, we can exclaim: "The great mystery of Christianity is not exactly the appearance but the transparence of God in the universe. Ah, yes, Lord, not only the ray that breaks the surface but the ray that penetrates; not your epiphany, Jesus, but your diaphany" *(The Divine Milieu).*

The Indicatory and Revelatory Functions of the Sacramental Realm

The transparence of the world with respect to God is what enables us to understand sacramental structure and sacramental thinking. It tells us that God is never reached directly in and by self. We always reach God together with the world and the things of the world, which are diaphanous and transparent with respect to God. Hence experience of God is always a sacramental experience. In things we experience God. The sacrament is part of the (immanent) world, but it holds within it another (transcendent) world: God. And insofar as it makes God present, it is part of that other world as well. Thus, we always find two movements in a sacrament: one running from God to the thing, the other running from the thing to God. So we can say that sacraments have two functions: an indicatory function and a revelatory function.

In its *indicatory function* a sacramental object points to God present within it. God is apprehended *in* the object, not *along with* the object. The object does not absorb the human being's gaze and attention; it allows the human being to look beyond it to the God present in it as a sacramental object. Human beings see the sacrament, but they must not rest their gaze there on the object. They must transcend the object and see the God communicated in the sacrament. Here we have the indicatory function of a sacrament, which moves from the object to God.

In its *revelatory function* a sacrament reveals, communicates, and expresses God present in it. The movement is from God to the sacramental object. God, who is invisible and intangible, becomes visible and tangible. God's ineffable presence in the object means that the latter becomes transfigured and diaphanous. Without ceasing to belong to this world, it becomes an instrument and vehicle of communication with God's world, the place of God's transparence and diaphany. People of faith are invited to immerse themselves in the divine light that now shines in the world.

A sacrament does not tear human beings away from this world. It addresses an appeal to them, asking them to look more closely and deeply into the very heart of the world. As Paul wrote in Romans 1:19-20, all human beings without exception are called to reflect deeply on the works of creation. No one is excluded or excused. If they do that tirelessly, the seemingly invisible realities of God's power and divinity will begin to become visible. The world, without ceasing to be world, will be transmuted into an eloquent sacrament of God. The essential vocation of human beings on earth is to become sacramental human beings.

When my Christmas candle is lit once a year for a few moments, it reminds me of two things. It points to a past event and it speaks to me of a sister's gesture to her brother. It rescues that happening from the mortality of the past and makes it alive in the present. Its flickering light reveals another light, a divine light, that was lit in the night of human abandonment and helplessness to tell us: Rejoice! The light is stronger than the darkness. This light is the true light enlightening every human being who comes into this world. It was already in the world. The world was already diaphanous and transparent, revealing God, but human beings did not see. Then, thanks to God's diaphany, we saw the bright radiance of God's glory, the glory of the only begotten Son of the Father, full of grace and truth (see Jn 1:9-14).

6

Life-Story as Sacrament

There are moments in life when consideration of the past becomes the truth of the present, revealing its deepest rationale and meaning. Seen close-up, the past actually ceases to be the past; it becomes the way in which we live the present. Some meaningful experience in the present opens up a whole new perspective for looking back at the past. The picture was there, but no one could see it because no one had the eyes. Then an experience in the present creates new eyes with which to see old things, and the old things become as new as the present.

The past now shows up, not as a soothing succession of happenings, but rather as a coherent, logical chain of events. A mysterious connection links the facts and events together. There surfaces a patent meaning that once lay submerged in the river of life. A plan was slowly unfolding, as one might unfold a map of some geographical territory. In the tangle of data we now discern cities, rivers, and the roads connecting major points. The territory is no longer *terra incognita.* Now mapped, it has meaning for the traveler, who can move forward without going astray because the route is visible.

Something like that happens in life. Points are established, paths are opened up. No one knows exactly where they may lead, but they are paths. Suddenly something of great importance happens. A point, akin to a big city, appears on the map of life. It is crisscrossed by highways, rivers, and airlines. Life begins to take on real meaning because we have a point to latch onto, a major elevation from which we can survey the surrounding landscape. A coherent course, a logical chain, has taken shape in our lives.

This sort of present is a very profound experience, entailing preparation, suffering, and the purification of crises. It has slowly ripened into maturity. A certain decision meant a commitment for one's whole life, meant salvation or damnation. We gave our word and took our stand vis-a-vis life. We cannot take back that word without changing the whole course of our existence. From the standpoint of that decision we look back at the past and reread everything in terms of it. We see how it was conceived, nurtured, shaped, and finally brought to birth. We read the meaning of our lives in terms of a past that culminates in the present and the decision made.

Let me be concrete and personal. On the night of December 14, 1964, eighteen young men, age twenty-six, chose to be ordained priests. I was one of them. Tomorrow would be the day of our ordination. The preparation for it had taken fifteen years. Tomorrow I would put on Christ again, invested with the power and authority to represent him and to lend him my presence, my voice, my actions, my body. It makes one tremble to probe and ponder the significance of such mysterious audacity, to take cognizance of the abyss that separates sinner from holy one. In the game of life I would be playing the role of Christ. It would be an absolutely serious matter, as is the case in any game.

The priestly ordination took place. We survived the eruption of the divine mystery. A week later we celebrated our first Mass, at least our first Mass among relatives and friends in our homeland. They all came, their eyes filled with respect. Primitive archetypes were activated. Everybody was afraid to get too close to the one who had been consecrated to God. But the archetypes of family and familiarity broke the taboo. The comments began, voiced mainly by the older aunts and women who had nestled the baby, now ordained a priest, in their laps and had witnessed his early boyish pranks: "I always said that he had shown an inclination to the priesthood even as a little boy. He was celebrating Masses when he was five, dressed in an old cape, and he was giving sermons to his little brother and sisters!" An old employee recalled: "Once he climbed atop a tree stump and gave a sermon in the Capuchin style. He condemned his brother to hell and the other reacted sharply. He fell and a thorn went through his leg. I think he even had to have some surgery on it!" Everyone was linking facts and events together, creating the chain that would take final shape with priestly ordination and this Mass today.

I myself can only recall the day of May 9, 1949. Until that day I had never thought of being a priest. There was a healthy tradition of anticlericalism in my family, a precious heritage that we all still cherish to this day. That particular day I saw a priest. He was from Rio de Janeiro and he was giving us a talk on vocations to the priesthood. He spoke of St. Francis and St. Anthony, of the grandeur of being another Christ on earth. He wound up with this: "Those who want to be priests, raise your hands!" I heard every word he said and felt an incredible glow of heat, which rushed to my face. The brief moment between his proposal and my response seemed like an eternity. Someone inside me raised my hand. My name was taken down and my father was notified. At home, later, I bemoaned my action. Why would I want to be a priest? I wanted to be a truck driver. That seemed the grandest job in the world: to control and drive those big monsters over our old highways. But my word had been given, my life defined.

I entered the seminary. The links of the chain began to be forged. On the night of December 14, 1964, I would finally unite them. My God, what a chain they made! I can still hear the echo of the words we all pronounced: "Lord, with joy and simplicity of heart, I have offered you everything . . ." And the congregation answered: "Preserve this holy resolution of his, O Lord."

Life is made up of rereadings of the past. Each important decision in the present opens up new perspectives on the past. Each event that has taken place takes on meaning as a guiding thread secretly carrying a future now rendered present. Past fact anticipates, prepares, symbolizes the future. It assumes a sacramental character.

Human History a Sacrament

All things are sacraments when viewed in God's perspective and light. The world, human beings, and things are signs and symbols of the transcendent.

For the early church, human history was particularly a sacrament. In history it saw the carrying out of God's salvation plan, the acceptance or rejection of God's grace by human beings. The meaning of events also bore a transcendent meaning, fleshing out God's saving plan. The history of barbarous actions and the antihistory of the humiliated and unjustly oppressed were expressions of the human "no" to God's salvific call. Facts and events became so many images of salvation or damnation, sacraments signifying and rendering present those alternatives. With unified meaning, all history assumed a sacramental character.

The concrete acts of that history also take on a sacramental character, even the humdrum acts of daily life. The struggle of a people for liberation becomes a sacrament. The labor movement and its struggle to win basic rights with blood and sweat, the activities of community groups to gain and celebrate the installation of basic utilities and public services: all these things flesh out a bit more the reign of God and anticipate definitive salvation.

The Hebrew people were masters at interpreting human history as a history of salvation or damnation. On the basis of some very important experience, they continually reread their whole past history. New syntheses arose, in which their present was found implicitly announced and slowly prepared way back in the past. It gradually emerged into the light and then broke clear in their present experience of faith. The past was a sacrament of the present.

Let me give examples of this. In the reigns of David and Solomon, the Israelites finally conquered Canaan. There was peace and tranquility of order. Around 950 B.C.E., under King Solomon, two great theologians of history arose. One was the Yahwist, so called because he always called God "Yahweh" in his writings. He interpreted the present peace as the incarnation of God's peace for his people. From that present he read the past as God's way of preparing and moving towards the happy situation of the present.

The present was not an accident. It was the product of God's loving plan for the people of Israel. The Yahwist then elaborated a vigorous religious synthesis. God had created everything, and everything was good. Humanity lived in the atmosphere of God's love, symbolized in the garden of delights or the earthly paradise. But humanity fell and God scattered its members all over the earth. A new beginning was vainly attempted with Noah. Then God chose Abraham to be the instrument of salvation for all peoples. He promised him Canaan as a land for the chosen people born of Abraham. The chosen people, however, came to be enslaved in Egypt. God liberated them from Egypt and permitted them to undertake the gradual conquest of the Canaanite region and culture. This plan was finally realized with David and Solomon.

The road had been long and full of detours. But God wrote straight with crooked lines. The present permitted the Yahwist to reread the whole past in the light of the present.

Two hundred years later, the situation was very different. The unity of David's and Solomon's kingdom was no more.

The Northern Kingdom was now threatened by the Assyrians. Moral decadence prevailed. The promised land, so painstakingly conquered, was in danger of being invaded. Around 740 B.C.E., when this was the situation, another great theologian arose. He was the Elohist, so called because he used the name "Elohim" for God. His present situation gave him a perspective from which to reread the past as a slow journey toward national disaster. He did not see the past as a history of salvation but rather as a history of damnation. His vision was thus very different from that of the Yahwist.

The Elohist's synthesis was very simple. God always has made a covenant with his people. The people break the covenant, God punishes them, and then he renews the covenant. The people continue to betray the covenant, so that the latter becomes a symbol of their betrayal and rejection of God. Israel can be happy and escape the Assyrian threat only by becoming faithful to God again. The events of the past are so many sacraments of Israel's present infidelity. The present situation is the product of a whole history of betrayals by Israel.

A Sacrament Shaped with Each Rereading

The Bible is full of such rereadings. The New Testament is the ultimate major rereading of all past history. To the apostles and evangelists the death and resurrection of Jesus Christ offered a definitive light on how to decipher the hidden meaning of the past. For them, as for us, the risen Jesus Christ was the crucial and decisive fact for humanity, showing that liberation from death, the limitations of life, and historical absurdity was indeed possible. This event was not an accident or a miscarriage. It had been prepared in history, had been gestating within creation. As St. Augustine would say later, history was pregnant with Christ. He was growing toward birth.

We can reread the whole past from the standpoint of Christ, as did the New Testament. The whole of creation is already oriented toward him. Adam is the image and likeness of Christ.

40

Christ was secretly present in Abraham, Moses, and Isaiah. He spoke through the mouths of Budda, Chuang-Tzu, Socrates, and Plato. Their significance is fully revealed in the light of Christ. Jesus accomplished in reality what they had in mind. They are sacraments of Christ.

Later, Christians had the personal experience of ecclesial community as a community of love, unity, service, and hope. This present fact gave them a perspective from which to reread the past again. We can see the result in such witnesses as Papias, the *Didache*, Tertullian, Origen, and St. Augustine. Christians of the first few centuries after Christ saw the church being prepared with Adam and Eve at the start of creation. Adam and Eve had formed the first community of love. The religions of the world, the people of Israel, and the apostolic community made up of Jesus and the Twelve were so many sacraments and symbols of the church. The church had been gradually prepared for its full manifestation at Pentecost.

There is one final way to do a sacramental reading of history. One can view everything in terms of the ultimate end and goal of history, in terms of heaven or hell. Then everything becomes a sacrament paving the way for the final end, including creation, all nations, all religions, all political communities, Jesus Christ, and the church. They are penultimate links and anticipatory symbols of the end. When the end finally comes, as the *Imitation of Christ* reminds us, the function of the sacraments will cease. We shall see face-to-face, no longer needing the mediation of signifying symbols.

It is obvious that this reading is not arbitrary. Human life is a rereading of the past, a way to live the present and gain strength for the future. A newly ordained priest rereads his whole past history from the standpoint of his ordination, which is a major event in his life. He discovers countless little insignificant acts

41

that anticipated and foreshadowed the future that is now his present. They all become symbols and sacraments for him. And so it is with human history. It is a sacrament of liberation or oppression, of salvation or damnation.

7

A Schoolteacher as Sacrament

He was practically a myth. To the inhabitants of the interior, where the mass media and their superstars had not yet arrived, he was considered a hero, a wise man, a master, and a counselor. His word became a proverb, his solution the right way.

Who was this mortal? Mr. Mansueto, the elementary schoolteacher in Planalto, Santa Catarina, a small town populated by Italian settlers. To those of us who knew him and were his pupils he was the sacramental symbol of life's fundamental values: idealism, abnegation, humility, love of neighbor, wisdom about life. Values are not communicated by proclaiming them or defending them in the abstract. They are communicated by living them concretely and relating them to individuals whose lives incarnate them.

Mr. Mansueto was one of those living apparitions. Perhaps with the passage of years our minds tend to turn past experiences into myth: but in the case of our beloved schoolteacher myth may well be the best way to preserve the richness of his simple, concrete life and story. In our town he stood out as does a pine tree amid grasslands or rolling pastures.

More than anything else, Mr. Mansueto was an idealist. He had been educated in the humanities in a strict old seminary. He had taken courses in accounting and a correspondence course in law back in the days when that was still possible. He had studied many other subjects. That frail, thin man of rustic elegance, with his fine, intelligent head, had left everything behind to teach in the rural wilderness, to free the first pioneers of our interior area from their ignorance and forlorn helplessness.

To us he always remained something of a mystery. In a world without any culture, he had a library of almost two thousand books. He lent them out to everybody, compelling the settlers and their children to read them. He studied the Latin classics in the original language, spent his spare time with such thinkers as Spinoza, Hegel, and Darwin, and subscribed to the *Correio do Povo* of Porto Alegre. He gave morning and afternoon classes, and at night he taught older people, anticipating Mobral. Along with all that he ran a class for brighter students, giving them a course in accounting. He formed a group that discussed political and cultural issues. The great problems of society and metaphysics preoccupied the restless soul of that anonymous thinker living in an insignificant town of the interior. Sometimes we former students of his, at this point attending the university, would ask him to take our place at home sessions on problems of constitutional law, the legitimacy of using force to achieve a victorious revolution, or general topics of our nation's history. How delighted he would be to hear that we were making top grades in our university courses!

That was the man who had been our teacher in primary school. There he taught us our first Greek and Latin words, our first rudimentary snatches of philology. How proudly we recited those words later in high school! In class he transmitted to us all that a person, educated only at that primary university, needed to know: principles of ecology, rights and justice, land measurement, civil legislation, house construction, and religion as a vision of God in the world around us.

When the radio went on the market, he got sets and compelled the settlers to buy them. He himself set them up in order to open their minds to the wide horizons of the world. Most of the settlers spoke Italian, a few spoke German; now they could learn Portuguese and become members of the human world at large. When some people refused to take the radio into their home, he had an effective alternative. He would set the radio on top of a pole in front of their house, turn the volume up full blast, and walk away. When penicillin was democratized, it was he who saved dozens of lives, some of which had already been given up as hopeless by medical doctors. His reputation grew to the point where the inhabitants put blind faith in his prescriptions, which he got from technical works on the subject, and in the remedies that he bought in distant pharmacies. He acted as the lawyer for native Indians and Blacks, who were objects of fierce discrimination on the part of the immigrant population. How often we heard them say: "God in heaven and Mr. Mansueto on earth!"

He died at an early age, worn out by his many labors on behalf of his large family and everybody else. He knew that he was going to die. His weary heart told him so. He welcomed death as a friend and dreamed of holding heavenly conversations with the great sages and asking God all the big questions. His death came about a thousand kilometers away from the area. The people went and claimed his body. The rest was an apotheosis. A real Mansuetology began to take shape. People began to remember and interpret his life, his words, his actions, augmenting rather than inventing him. They idealized and magnified him, turning him into their symbol and type of a humanity consecrated to others down to the last self-consuming ounce.

My dear readers, if some day you should happen to pass through a tiny but laughing city with the name Concórdia and visit the cemetery there, and if you happen across a grave on the left with a pretty couplet, ever fresh flowers, and memento offerings by the large cross, that is the grave of schoolteacher Mansueto. And he still lives in the memory of those people.

For the early church as for us today, a sacrament did not have to be some object in the world, for example, a mug, a loaf of bread, a Christmas candle. As we have already noted, history itself could be a sacrament. The meaning of events could convey a radical meaning called salvation, or a meaninglessness hinting at a more profound absurdity interpreted as damnation. In history appear persons who embody and increase the meaning of history, who incarnate liberation, grace, goodness, and unbounded openness to others and the great Other. The Fathers called those historical figures sacraments: Abraham, Noah, David, Sarah, Rebecca, Anna, Mary, and the like. I myself would add Mr. Mansueto.

In this line of thinking, Jesus of Nazareth is called the Sacrament *par excellence* by virtue of his life, his acts of kindness, his courageous death, and his resurrection. In him the history of salvation found its culmination as the realization of Meaning. He first arrived at the end of the long process of humanization, overcame death, and burst through into the Mystery of God. Jesus of Nazareth appears as the fontal sacrament of God insofar as he incarnates the saving plan of God, that is, the complete and total union of the creature with the Creator, and shows us, by way of anticipation, the ultimate destiny of all redeemed human beings.

If God is love and pardon, the servant of the whole human creature and gracious sympathy for all human beings, then Jesus Christ embodies God in our midst through his inexhaustible capacity for love, his complete renunciation of the will to power and revenge, and his identification with those marginalized by this world and its order. The gestures, actions, and phases of Christ's life were sacraments that concretized the Mystery of God. The Fathers spoke of the mysteries and sacraments of the flesh of Christ *(mysteria et sacramenta carnis Christi)*. From him we get grace upon grace (Jn 1:16). In him was Life (Jn 1:4); he was the Life (Jn 11:25; 14:6). In and with Jesus of Nazareth appeared the goodness and loving kindness of God, our Savior (Tit 3:4; 2 Tim 1:10). He was the visible form of the invisible God (Col 1:15), the irruption and epiphany of the divinity in the diaphany of visible, palpable flesh (Col 2:9; 1 Jn 1:2). "Whoever has seen me has seen the Father" (Jn 14:9). It is in this sense that the great tradition of the church, right up to and including Vatican II, calls Christ the sacrament of God. Mr. Mansueto was a sacrament of the values that Jesus of Nazareth lived down to their very roots and incarnated with crystal clarity.

Jesus Christ, Sacrament of the Encounter with God

God's encounter with humanity is marked in all things. In them the human being can encounter God. All the things of this world are or can be sacramental.

Christ is the meeting place *par excellence.* In him God has a human form and the human being has a divine form. The Christian faith has always seen and believed that in the dead and resurrected Jesus of Nazareth God and the human being meet in a profound unity without division or confusion. Through the human Jesus one goes to God, and through the God-Jesus one goes to human beings. He is the way and the destination of the journey. In him the two movements of ascent and descent meet. On the one hand he is the palpable expression of God's love (descent); on the other hand he is the definitive form of human love (ascent). Whoever dialogued with Christ was having an encounter with God.

Whenever my memory goes back to Mr. Mansueto, I see more than Mr. Mansueto. I see a sacrament. He made visible and historical what was greater than himself: abnegation, love for neighbor, utmost dedication. If one looks even farther, he mediated the One who was Abnegation itself, radical Love for neighbor and total Dedication. Because he was a sacrament.

47

8

Home as Sacrament

We obviously do not travel just to arrive. But on a journey the arrival is the best part. I am thinking of the return trip to home. Arriving is like anchoring safely and securely in port after having gone through all sorts of potential perils. There are so many who travel and never arrive.

Arrival is so good because human beings don't live for long without a home or away from home. Home is the portion of the world that has become familiar and sacramental. There each thing has its own place and meaning. Nothing is foreign, everything is perfectly familiar. The things in a home possess life and dwell with human beings. That is why there is nothing more terrible than those huge houses that are useless and empty. They are not familiar. They have no household gods. The things in them are not kindly spirits but mere things, possessed for the sake of vanity and ostentation. They are not alive. Hence the home of the vainly affluent becomes a sinister place.

Only those who have had to live away from their paternal, familiar home really know what such a home means. I did so for years on end, returning home suddenly in 1970. The fringes of my native Brazil suddenly appeared in the distance as I stood on the ship. My heart beat faster with excitment and affection. As the ship drew closer to shore, I became enveloped in the folds of familiarity. Fear was banished. Even death seemed sweet. Yes, even death would be okay here and now because I would be dying in the familiar, welcoming arms of my native country. I land! There are the warm welcomes and many embraces. Then we are on the road that will take us to our Franciscan home. I look at everything, examining and scrutinizing it as one would an old friend: the mountain range in the distance, the trees, the curves of the road.

Finally we reach the house. To be more exact: the monastery, the family home of all the Franciscan friars. It is the same as it had been. The world and I had turned and changed, but it was still planted firmly there on a slight rise of ground. After embracing everybody, I wanted to see every corner of the house. Everything in it was important: "This was the room where . . ." One room was the place where I had studied hard. Another was the chapel. We got up early in those days and fought a terrible battle with drowsiness as we prayed and tried to come to grips with God and pick a bone with Jesus Christ. And over there was the dim library, and the corridor called Paradise, and the narrow cell in which I lived.

Now we have to go outside! I must say hello to the trees, greet the lanes around the hill, and say a prayer to the Virgin Mary in the grotto as I once did every day at 9:30 A.M.

Everything becomes familiar once again. How good it is to be able to say: Home at last! As I say it, the depths of my soul reverberate with all the archetypal resonances of cozy shelter, spontaneity, simplicity, and the joy of being surrounded by familiar things.

The whole house, you see, is one big sacrament, and everything in it shares its sacramental nature. Its objects and parts become sacraments too: the recreation room, the refectory, the bedrooms, the library, the pictures on the walls, the statues, the foliage on the garden walk, the old staircases. Everything is somehow sacred and sacramental. You do not violate a home because it is a sanctuary. You do not invite just anyone into a home because it has a sacramental nature. Only those who have been initiated into our friendship and love can truly savor with us the family intimacy of all things in the house.

When we think about it, we realize that our home is a concentrated and fontal sacrament. Starting from its precincts, other things also become sacramental in an ever widening circle: our city, our local region, our state, our native country, our continent. Eventually the planet earth itself becomes sacramental for an astronaut on the moon. Astronaut James Irwin noted that the moon was beautiful and space deep and wondrous. But only the green planet below him offered a welcoming vision because on it was someone who was thinking of him and waiting for him.

Our home as a fontal sacrament keeps opening up to embrace ever wider circles of reality. If and when human beings travel out beyond the solar system, it may well be that the whole solar system will become sacramental for them. It will be different from any other system because within it lie the earth, a continent, a native land, a state, a local region, a city, and a family home.

Because of this old house I am in, with its dim corridors, narrow cells, Franciscan austerity, and no running water, some space traveler will fix all attention some night on the planet earth, where the whole meaning of the universe is concentrated. A sacrament, you see, can open up to embrace everything; it all depends on our openness of heart.

The Church, Sacrament of Christ

The church in its totality as the community of the faithful and of the history of their faith in the risen Jesus Christ—with its creed, its liturgy, its canon law, its customs and traditions, its saints and martyrs—has always been called the great sacrament of grace and salvation in the world. Within it the church

51

carries the precious gift of Jesus Christ, who is the fontal sacrament of God. As Christ was the sacrament of the Father, so the church is the sacrament of Christ. He continues on and becomes palpable in history through the church. The church keeps ever alive the memory of his life, death, and resurrection, and of his definitive significance for the destiny of all human beings.

Without the church, Christ would still act in history. He would be present in the process of human liberation. He would secretly reach the hearts of all because he is infinitely greater than the church. He is not the church's divine prisoner. But if there were no church, no community of believers, there would be no one to draw him out of anonymity, to decipher his present but hidden reality, to pronounce his true name, and to venerate him as the Liberator of human beings and Lord of the cosmos. The church becomes a sacrament insofar as it participates in, and daily actualizes, the sacrament of Christ. In its historical concreteness it serves as a familial and sacramental home for people of faith. The four walls are not what turns a house into a familial and sacramental home. Nor is it the empty space in it that gives us room to dwell there. That transformation is effected by the spirit of the person who fills the empty house with life and confers meaning on the four walls. Only then is the house habitable and familiar.

And so it is with the church. The creed, the liturgy, the institutions and traditions are not the things that make the church what it is, the sacrament of Christ. It is faith in the Lord and his presence that gives life to the creed, finds expression in the liturgy, is incarnated in its institutions, and is alive in its traditions. All that forms the sacrament, that is, the instrument with which the invisible Lord in heaven makes himself visible on earth. Within and behind the sensible signs (sacraments) lies hidden the true salvific reality of the church: Jesus Christ and his mystery. The church possesses structures as other societies do. It has laws and doctrines as they do, even as it has order, discipline, and morality. But the church is different from other societies because of the Spirit that animates it.

In our sacramental family home there are rooms, halls, tables, and pictures on the wall just as there are in other houses. But they are different because the spirit that invests them with affection and meaning is different, and it makes them familiar and sacramental. No one can see a difference from the outside. Only the heart knows and sees it. And so it is with the church. In the church's fragile and often contradictory outward appearances only faith discovers and recognizes an inner, divine secret: the presence of the risen Lord. That is why the Church Fathers often called the church a wondrous and ineffable sacrament (*mirabile et ineffabile sacramentum*).

As the fontal sacrament, Christ was human and divine, so in an analogous way the universal sacrament, the church, is also human and divine. (It is not so in exactly the same way because there is no hypostatic union in the church.) The divine element is always incarnated in the human element, making the latter transparent. The human element is in the service of the divine element, making the latter historical. Thus, the church is really more a living organism than an organization, a community of salvation rather than an institution of salvation.

Everything in the Church Is Sacramental

If the church as a great, united whole is one big sacrament, then so are all the things in it. All the things in the church are sacamental because they recall Christ or give concreteness to the church as sacrament: the liturgy with its rites, sacred objects, books, and material elements; the people, from the pope down to the lowliest member; the activity of the church in the world, including social assistance, missionary work, and prophetic proclamation. In the eyes of the Church Fathers, even the dismissal of a bishop and the profession of a religious were considered sacramental. All the gestures, acts, and words of the church as sacrament take on an equally sacramental function. In the concrete reality of life they give specificity to the nature of the church as a sacrament.

Just as all places can take on sacramental dimensions from the starting point of the sacramental family home, as we noted above, so it is in the case of the church. As the bearer of grace and sacrament of Jesus Christ, the church's presence is realized wherever Christ and his grace reach. Christ has cosmic dimensions; he penetrates and embraces everything. The church, too, embraces and penetrates everything. One of the earliest Christian texts, the *Didache*, rightly noted that the church is "a cosmic mystery." The church is limited only in its signs and its historical humanity. The mystery that penetrates all those signs and all that historical humanity is free; it can make its presence felt in all the phases of the world. That is why the Church Fathers could talk about the cosmic church, the church of natural law, the church of the world's religions, the church of Judaism, the church of Jesus Christ, the church of the apostles, and the glorious church in heaven where "all the just from the time of Adam, from Abel . . . to the last of the elect, will be gathered together" (*Lumen gentium*, n. 2).

My old Franciscan home, for all its limitations, is good to live in, good to come back to. From there the world takes on meaning, and the streets a certain direction. So it is with the church. It is very old and weighed down by the centuries. Its hands are often callous in dealing with human beings. It is often much too prudent. It is slow to move because it is slow to understand. Despite all these faults, however, it is in the church that we were conceived, born, nurtured, and raised. It is in the church that we daily and always encounter Jesus Christ, and with him all things. Because the church is the sacrament of Christ.

9

The Sacramental Axes of Life

In our family home, which is a sacrament, everything is sacramental. But there are various degrees of sacramental concentration and density. There is mama's and papa's room, for example. All the objects are sacramental, but a certain mug is a special sacrament. Everything is holy, but there is a holy of holies. There are also special moments at home when its whole sacramental nature finds concentrated expression and becomes transparent. Family meals used to be such for us, and they still continue to be. We ate only when the whole family was at the table. How often we waited up to an hour for some member to get there! Eating is not something done just to satisfy our physical hunger. Eating is done with the eyes and heart as well. We nurture not only our body but also our spirit, family union, and cozy closeness. The family meal is a total sacrament, strengthening the bonds of affection and turning many lives into one life: a family life.

Every day is the same as the next; it has twenty-four hours. But one's birthday is different. It is sacramental because it celebrates the greatest miracle of all. On that day you began to live and you are alive now! One's birthday, then, is filled with symbols and rites that make it different from every other day.

On wedding anniversaries people celebrate the beginning of a history of love and the love of their personal history. They do not simply recall the past, however; they continually actualize it anew. They reinforce the present so as to guarantee the fu-

55

ture. It is a sacramental day; the flowers, the presents, and the special meal take on an eminently sacramental function.

Why Seven Sacraments?

If everything in the church is sacramental, why are there seven sacraments? This is a legitimate question, and we can try to answer it on two levels.

First, we may look at the level of conscious history. Up till the twelfth century the word "sacrament" was used as I have been using it here. In this, the oldest tradition of the church, it was used for everything having to do with the sacred. In the twelfth century theologians began to pinpoint seven primoridal acts of the church among the hundreds of "sacraments." St. Augustine, for example, had enumerated 304 sacraments. The new focus on seven began to appear with such theologians as Rudulfus Ardens (d.1200), Otto of Bamberg (d.1139), and Hugh of St. Victor (d.1141).

These seven primoridal acts are our seven sacraments today. The church officially adopted this doctrine at the Synod of Lyons in 1274 and the Council of Florence in 1439. Finally, in 1547 the Council of Trent solemnly declared: "The sacraments of the new law are seven, no more and no less, i.e., baptism, confirmation, the eucharist, penance, extreme unction, holy orders, and matrimony" (Session VII, Canon 1).

This is the explanation on the level of conscious history and actual fact, and it is legitimate. But it does not suffice. It does not provide the why and wherefore of the seven sacraments or explain their meaning. It is a positivistic explanation: there are seven sacraments because the church decided that and Jesus Christ wanted it!

Understanding something does not mean merely listing data but seeing the connection between them and detecting the in-

56

visible structure underlying them. That structure is not on the surface. It lies on a deeper level, revealing itself through the surface facts. We must descend there through the data and then come up again to understand the data. Such is the process of all real knowledge, whether in science or theology.

This brings us to our second level: the unconscious, structural level. If we try to see the seven sacraments on this deeper level, we shall find their true significance. The choice of seven sacraments, made consciously in the twelfth century, was not arbitrary. It articulated the deeper meaning embodied in the sacramental rites and in the symbolic, archetypal character of the number seven.

If we look closely, we shall see that on the ritual level the seven sacraments express the pivotal points of human life. There are key moments in life, especially in its biological dimensions. There are nodal points in life where the crucial lines of the transcendent meaning of the human being meet and cross. At these points human beings sense that their lives are not self- sustaining. They possess life, but they have received it. They sense that they are immersed in the current of life that passes through the world and the community. They realize that they never simply live by themselves but rather *with* others. They receive life from a field of rice and beans, from a supply of water, from a small handful of people who have welcomed them into the world and now support and love them despite their pettiness, thus enabling them to believe that life is worth living.

In these key moments we experience our participation in a force that transcends us but is also manifested in our lives. These nodal points in life take on an eminently sacramental character, and so we surround them with symbols and rites. This is true even in the most secularized sort of life. These nodal points are the sacraments of life *par excellence* because in them is transparently condensed the life of the sacraments: the presence of the Transcendent, of God. The external rites flesh out the deeper, underlying experience that may even be unconscious. Where life is personally experienced in a radical way, there God is experienced.

The moment of birth is a key moment in life. The newborn baby is there as sheer gratuitousness. Its acceptance into the family and continued survival depend on the good will of others. Baptism displays and develops this dependence as dependence on God, and sublimely enhances it as participation in the life of Christ.

Another key moment in life is the moment when the child, now grown and free, makes up its own mind. It is mature and takes its place in adult society and the work force. It is an important turning point in life, in which a person's destiny is at stake to some extent. Once again human beings sense that they are dependent on a higher Force. They experience God. The sacrament of confirmation is the sacrament of Christian adulthood. It spells out the God dimension present in this pivotal point of life.

Without food life cannot be maintained. Every meal permits human beings to have the gratifying experience that their being is linked to other beings. This is why human eating is surrounded with rites. The eucharist displays the latent meaning of eating as participation in the divine life itself.

Another pivotal point in life is marriage. The life of love is one of mutual gratuitousness. The bonds uniting the pair are fragile because they depend on their freedom. The two people experience something that escapes the human realm: the guarantee of fidelity. It depends on, calls for, a higher force: God. The sacrament of matrimony spells out the presence of God in love.

Illness can threaten human life. Sick people sense their

limitedness and again experience their dependence. The sacrament of the anointing of the sick expresses the healing and saving power of God.

We all have the profound experience of guiltily breaking with other human beings and with God. We feel divided and lost. We are anxious for redemption and reconciliation with everything. The sacrament of penance, of return, spells out the experience of pardon and the meeting between the prodigal son and the forgiving father.

We want to live in a reconciled world rather than in a broken one, to be able to achieve universal reconciliation and peace. This is the secret desire underlying and inspiring our quest for happiness. The sacrament of holy orders anoints people to live this reconciliation and consecrates them to serve the community in the task of fashioning reconciliation.

When theologians in the twelfth century decided on the number of the fundamental rites of the faith, they were moved by the collective unconscious of life and the faith. The church as sacrament extends its activity over the whole of life, but it does so in different ways. It presents itself at the key moments of existence, making explicit the presence of God who graciously accompanies us. These are the essential rites of the faith, which give reality and actuality to the very essence of the church as a sign of salvation in the world. Once the essence of the church is made real, theology can detect it and specify it. It can determine the essential sacraments of the faith are seven. The principal sacraments of the faith are made concrete in the principal and pivotal points of human life. Life is replete with grace.

What Does the Number Seven Signify?

The Council of Trent defined that there are seven sacraments, no more and no less. But we must understand this definition. The essential element in it is not the number seven, but the rites included in the enumeration. The precise number of the rites is not the essential thing. If someone were to say that there are nine sacraments because the diaconate and the episcopate are real sacraments, that would not be a denial of Trent's definition. Nor would it be a denial to say that there are six sacraments because baptism and confirmation form one single sacrament of initiation at different levels. But one would have to say that confirmation is a sacrament, and that all these rites render present and communicate the grace of God.

The number seven must be understood symbolically—not as the sum of 1 plus 1 plus 1 and the like, but as the result of 3 plus 4. Depth psychology, structuralism, and the Bible and tradition long before them, tell us that the numbers 3 and 4, added together, are the specific symbol of the totality of an ordered plurality.

The number 4 is the symbol of the cosmos (with its four elements: earth, air, fire, and water), of movement, and of immanence. The number 3 is the symbol of the Absolute (the Holy Trinity), of spirit, of rest, and of transcendence. The sum of both, the number 7, signifies the union of the immanent and the transcendent, the synthesis of movement and rest, and the meeting of God and humanity (that is, the incarnate Word of God, Jesus Christ). With the number 7 we are trying to express the fact that the totality of human existence with its material and spiritual dimensions is consecrated by the grace of God. Salvation is not restricted to seven channels of communication. The totality of salvation is communicated to the totality of human life, and it is manifested in a significantly tangible way in the pivotal points of life. This is the fundamental meaning of the number seven.

Whenever we plunge into the depths of our life and existence—seeing it emerge at birth, grow, preserve itself, multiply, undergo consecration, healing from ruptures, and the like—we do not simply touch the mystery of life. We also penetrate into that dimension of absolute Meaning we call God and its manifestation in the world we call Grace. The sacrament is realized at the juncture of life with Life. Life vivifies life because of the sacrament.

10

Jesus Christ as Author of the Sacraments

The new face of the church is indisputably associated with the figure of Pope John XXIII. Vatican II, which established the theological guideposts for church reform, was the fruit of his commitment and action. Future historians will surely talk about the era of John XXIII. They will point to him as the author of a new and courageous large-scale attempt to incarnate the Christian faith in the spirit of modernity. He was its true author in the strict sense of the word: not of every action that was taken after him but of the horizon that made possible the new orientation of the church. Thus, he was the author of the ecumenical spirit, of open dialogue between the church and the world, of a simple, jovial spirit of service devoid of all traces of triumphalism, of a positive religious valuation of all the real and authentic things that modern civilization has produced, and so forth.

Similarly, Pope Paul VI was the author of the famous encyclical *Populorum progressio.* It is not that he wrote this crucial document with his own hand. He might not have had sufficient technical training and expertise to do that. We know that the written document itself was authored by Father Lebret and his group. Nevertheless we say with good reason that Paul VI was the author of that encyclical. It bears his signature and the official seal of his supreme authority. He is its author because he ultimately originated the whole process that culminated in that social encyclical. He is its author because he took responsibility for the message contained in the document and conferred his official authority on it.

President Vargas was the author of the Brazilian revolution of the 1930s. He was the author of a new era in our nation's history. It was characterized by such things as industrialization, nationalism, populism, and the achievement of fundamental rights for the working class (a minimum wage, unionism, social security, and so forth). Vargas was the author: not because he performed or engineered all those revolutionary actions but because he created the atmosphere and course that led to these profound changes in the sociopolitical shape of Brazil.

The Sacraments Were Instituted by Jesus Christ (Trent)

The Council of Trent solemnly defined that the Christian sacraments had been instituted by Our Lord Jesus Christ (DS 1601; see 1804, 2536). This statement is fundamentally correct; but it must be correctly understood in the sense that Trent gave it. For whole epochs theological reflection, which is still amply reflected in the manuals, took this statement of Trent in its merely syntactic sense. It made no effort to gain a deeper understanding of its precise semantic and pragmatic import. Theologians would simply look in the pages of the New Testament to find some statement by Christ supporting the institution of each one of the seven sacraments. Violence was done to the texts. But people's minds were no more enlightened afterwards, for all the sharpness and subtlety of theological reasoning.

Linking up with the most ancient tradition of the Church Fathers, modern theology has expanded the horizon in which the sacraments are to be pondered and comprehended. It claims to have found the real reasons enabling it to reaffirm the authorship of Jesus Christ with respect to the sacraments. Let us take a brief look at this matter.

The sacraments should not be considered in themselves as isolated atoms. A specific sacrament, baptism, for example, gives body and destiny to the "sacrament of the Father's will"

(Eph 1:9): that is, the economy of salvation, God's saving plan, the one and only mystery-sacrament, to use the phrase of such Church Fathers as St. Leo the Great, St. Cyprian, and St. Augustine. God's saving plan, called sacrament or mystery, is mediated in gestures, rites, or actions that incarnate, make visible, and communicate salvation. These actions, rites, and gestures are also called sacraments. Insofar as this saving plan has the eternal, preexistent Word as its author, we can say that all the sacraments ultimately derive from the eternal Word. The sacramental expressions are historical and cultural. Human beings express themselves through them. But the salvific force contained in them derives from the eternal Word. In this sense all sacraments are Christian sacraments, as St. Augustine astutely perceived. This includes the sacraments concocted by pagans in the world's religions. They, too, historicize the saving grace of God as well as the Father's loving plan that is realized in and through Jesus Christ, in whom all things exist and for whom all things were made (Col 1:15-20; Jn 1:3). The eternal Word was always at work, throughout the course of history. History is pregnant with Jesus Christ.

In terms of their ultimate reality, the pagan sacraments are not pagan. The notion of "pagan" is a sociological rather than a theological one. In sociological terms a pagan is one who has not been baptized and hence is not numbered among Christians in the statistics. But in theological terms there is no such thing as a pagan because no one escapes the influence of the eternal Word. The eternal Word is the true light that enlightens *every* human being who comes into the world (Jn 1:9). The Christian sacraments articulated in the world's religions pointed vertically to the eternal Word. They were sacraments of God. Eating was participating sacramentally in the deity. To undergo baptism was to immerse oneself in the divine life. Speaking generally, we can say that the sacraments we possess today in the church preexisted the church. Human beings of every age were sacramentally related to the deity (the eternal Word). The forms were different but the salvation communicated was the very same one that fully and infallibly wells up in the sacraments of the church.

When the sacraments of God (the eternal Word), which point vertically upward, are related to and inserted in the history of Jesus Christ, which registers horizontally as does any other history, then these sacraments become specifically Christian sacraments. The sacraments possess religious and cultural dimensions. They existed before the typically Christian explication. They were made up and elaborated historically. Even before the church there was baptism, whereby human beings manifested a rebirth required by the deity. Matrimony also existed, giving expression to the presence of divine Love in human love. The pivotal points of human life also existed before the church, and their sacramental density revealed the presence of the great Mystery. They were divine sacraments that were latently Christian.

Thanks to Jesus Christ, the Christian faith discovered the relationship of these sacraments to the incarnate God. It linked them to the mystery of the Word made human being. It incorporated them into the history that comes from Jesus Christ. The vertical dimension crossed paths with the horizontal dimension. The Christian sacrament is that encounter. On the one hand it presupposes and assumes the divine sacrament preexisting in human religions. On the other hand it discovers a reality that is present in the divine sacraments but hidden to the world's religions and now made manifest through the light of Christ's mystery: that is, the presence of the eternal Word who is acting through the divine sacraments. It also inserts these sacraments into the history of Jesus Christ in such a way that Christ assumes a specific authorship. Getting baptized no longer means participating in the life of the deity but immersing oneself in the life of Jesus Christ. Eating the sacred banquet no longer means partaking of the deity but eating the body of the Lord and participating in his resurrected life. Getting married no longer means symbolizing the union of God with human beings but representing the union of Christ with faithful humanity. The divine sacraments become explicitly Christian sacraments.

What Does This Mean?

From what has been said in the previous section, it should be clear in what sense Christ is to be considered the author of the sacraments. *First,* as the eternal Word, he was always the one communicating himself in love and salvation in the rites that expressed the relationship of human beings with the Most High. *Second,* as the eternal Word incarnate in a concrete history, he made clear that everything is linked to his Mystery. Hence everything has Christic depth. *Third,* in the case of three sacraments at least—baptism, the eucharist, and penance—Christ established an explicit reference to himself. These three sacraments relate to the pivotal points of human life, wherein human beings feel especially referred to the Transcendent and Jesus Christ. If we look closely we see that the three are at the roots of life itself. Baptism embodies our new life in Jesus Christ. The eucharist embodies the nurturing of this new life in Jesus Christ. Penance embodies the rebirth of that life after it has been threatened by fatal death.

Inserted in Jesus Christ, the sacraments communicate the life of Jesus Christ. The Council of Trent meant nothing else but that when it referred to the Lord's institution of the sacraments. It did not intend to offer a historical judgment or to supplant the efforts of exegetes. From the minutes and proceedings it is quite clear officially that Trent understood and meant the word "institute" in the following sense: Jesus Christ is the one who confers efficacy on the rite that is celebrated. Trent did not intend to define the institution of the rite but its saving force, the latter deriving not from the faith of the member or the community but from Jesus Christ, who is present.

Willing the church, the universal sacrament of salvation,

Christ also willed the sacraments that particularize the universal sacrament for the concrete realities of life. In that sense he wanted not only the seven sacraments but also the sacramental structure of the church. In other words, he wanted to see grace made visible in rites, gestures, and acts of service, witness, and sanctification in the midst of humanity. In this *fourth* sense we can call Christ the author of the sacraments insofar as he is the author of the universal sacrament, the church. The examples I gave at the start of this chapter (John XXIII, Paul VI, and Getúlio Vargas) may help to illuminate the horizon within which we also are to understand the authorship of Jesus Christ with respect to the sacraments.

Everything is Christ's. He did not just introduce something new: that is, himself and his resurrection. He also came to reveal the holiness of all things. All things are filled with him—yesterday, today, and always. What is specifically Christian is the capacity to see his activity and efficacy in all the articulations of human history, especially those wherein humanity most reveals itself as human. And Christian sacramentalism is specifically that because it knows enough to relate the "natural" sacraments to the mystery of Christ. Everything that is true, holy, and good is already Christian, even when the label "Christian" is not used. Nothing is rejected. Everything is taken over. Everything is read and interpreted in the light of the history of Christ's mystery. And so we get transfiguration: in its own specific and different way, each and every thing becomes a Christian sacrament. It comes from Christ and leads to Christ.

11

Promised Word as Sacrament

The spoken word is not primarily a means of communicating this or that to another person. Even before communicating messages, the spoken word communicates the person who is speaking. This word defines the person because a person is essentially communication. There are persons, few in number, who make that profound reality a matter of conscientious attention. They see their word as something absolutely sacred. The spoken word deserves respect because every person deserves respect. For the great majority of people, however, their word is nothing more than an instrument for communicating messages, self-serving messages, messages that sometimes pollute the channels of communication and encounter between human beings. There are words that are proffered to hide thoughts instead of communicating them.

Dr. Gomes is a very successful businessman. His affairs bring him into relations with people in the most diverse situations and with very differing interests. His whole way of being radiates profound serenity. He seems to be one of those Chinese mystics mounted gaily on a ferocious lion. In other words, he is a mature human being who has mastered his violent passions and turned them into constructuve forces. They now serve the project of a well-integrated human being. His words may be as tender and mild as drops of tender tears; but they may also be as harsh and cutting as any sword. Both the gentleness and harshness are in harmony, under the perfect control of a person who is master of the situation.

The most admirable thing about Dr. Gomes is the value and weight he gives to his words. His written word is crystal-clear; there is no ambiguity in it. When he writes, he enumerates his points: first . . . second . . . third. Here and there amid this mathematical clarity one finds a word or expression that communicates the person himself rather than messages, proposals, contracts, or facts: "Life is hard. It does not spare anyone. Authentic values come from the gracious benevolence of God and the humble, patient effort of human beings; those values should be able to see the light of day. We are here to serve." Benevolent light always manages to pierce the thickness of the forest and animate the plant life that insatiably seeks the sky.

For Dr. Gomes, his spoken word is even more important than the written word. His spoken word is his given word, history made. It costs him time and effort to utter his essential, deciding word. He consults with people, analyzes, takes plenty of time. He studies people and situations. Once he gives his word, everything is decided. He may lose money, be misunderstood, let slide contracts and documents that were in his own favor. His given word is sacred. It is a sacrament. It defines his person and can no longer be erased from space. Some people would argue that our spoken word is innocuous and empty because it gets lost in space and never returns. Dr. Gomes, on the other hand, sees the very same argument as one on behalf of the sacredness of one's given word. Once given as a promise, it goes out and circulates through the world. It is never lost because it reaches the Eternal and fixes a person in the Definitive.

The written word can be erased, wiped out, destroyed. The spoken word cannot. It is inviolable. No one has control over it any more. It is transcendent. Uttered in all one's personal solidity and maintained as one would maintain one's life and honor, it is supremely the sacrament that reveals and communicates each person as an individual. Dr. Gomes is what his word is: mature, honest, truthful, a creator of authentic communication. His word is what he is: effective, solid, weighty, decisive, a creator of acts that change life.

The Sacraments Work ex Opere Operato

From our reflections so far it should be obvious that a sacrament makes visible, communicates, and effects in reality what it signifies. Our family renders present the water that satisfied the thirst of all the family members. But it does more than that. Even today, because of its sacramental power, it accomplishes the same effect in all those people of whose history it was a part. Mama's homemade bread communicates and makes real what it signifies for the whole family. It satisfies not only our physical hunger but also our more basic hunger for fraternal communion and oneness. The water of baptism not only conveys purification and the life that is nurtured by water; it also speaks of the new life and purification that the mystery of Christ brought to human beings. The eucharistic bread not only makes visible the daily meal at the human table but also makes present, communicates, and realizes the bread of heaven, Jesus Christ, in the midst of the community of faith. And this takes place through the very presence of the bread, which evokes and thus renders present the heavenly banquet for people of faith.

The tradition of faith has always upheld the view that God's grace is infallibly present in the carrying out of the sacrament, so long as the action is performed with faith and the intention of communing with the universal community of believers. The presence of divine grace in the sacrament does not depend on the holiness of the one administering the sacrament or the one receiving it. Human beings and their merits are not the *cause* of grace. Only God and Jesus Christ are that. So when we say that a sacrament works *ex opere operato* we mean this: once the sacramental rite is performed, once the sacred symbols are employed, Jesus Christ is present and operative. This is not by virtue of the rites in and of themselves because they, as such, have no power; they merely symbolize. Jesus Christ is present and operative because of God's own promise. Otherwise, we would be caught up wholly in the realm of magic, where the view is that the sacred acts themselves possess a secret power that has a favorable or unfavorable effect on human beings.

A sacrament is profoundly different from magic. In the realm of the sacraments we believe that God takes over our human sacraments, such as those of bread and water, in order to produce an effect through them that goes beyond their own powers. Ordinary bread satisfies hunger and symbolizes family togetherness. In the eucharist God takes over this preexistent symbolism, elevates it to the divine dimension, and makes sure that this bread satisfies our human hunger for salvation and turns the new community of the redeemed into a reality. The phrase *ex opere operato* is ambiguous. It literally means "by virtue of the rite performed." But the church has never understood it in any ambiguous or magical terms. In negative terms the phrase means that the grace of the sacrament is not caused by any action or power of either its minister or its receiver; sacramental grace is caused by God. It is Christ who baptizes, pardons, consecrates. The ministers of the sacraments lend Christ their unworthy lips, their arms that can do wicked things, their bodies that can be instruments of wickedness. Grace is ever victorious when it becomes real in the world, whatever the situation of human beings may be. In positive terms *ex opere operato* means that once the sacred rite is enacted, we have a guarantee that God and Jesus Christ are present there.

Christ Is the Guaranteed Word of God to Humanity

This faith in the power of the sacraments, pivotal axes of life, has its roots in the data of christology and ecclesiology. The crucified and resurrected Jesus Christ is God's "Yes" and "Amen" to the promises made to humanity (see 2 Cor 1:19). In him and through him God accepted and pardoned us. Jesus is the guaranteed word of salvation that God gave each and every one of us. Before Christ, human beings lived with the hope that their lives and deaths would have a happy outcome. Thanks to the resurrection of Jesus Christ, they actually saw that God has accepted us in a decisive and definitive way. Fear was exorcised, threats dispelled. In Jesus Christ the victory of love and the triumph of grace were ensured forever.

As we have already noted, because Jesus Christ is all that, he can be considered and called the original and fontal sacrament of God and divine salvation. The church, as sacrament of Christ, prolongs and extends his sacramental reality throughout history. It preserves and maintains the mystery of Christ in all its concrete explication. The sacraments are acts of the church that touch human beings at the crucial moments in their lives. They make concrete and spell out the universal sacrament of the church. They make real the essence of the church in concrete life and its moments: for example, birth, maturation, nurturing, pardoning, loving, and dying. They are principally acts of Christ through his body, the church: acts with a permanent, definitive, sensible, and recognizable guarantee of grace to concrete human beings. This is wholly independent of human merit or demerit. God has spoken a categorical "Yes" to us. The term *ex opere operato* merely aims at pointing up this truth as emphatically as possible. God first loved us while we were still God's enemies. God's total and gratuitous love is to be found in Jesus Christ, the church, and the seven sacraments.

We are reminded of Dr. Gomes. When he gives his word, he invests all his honor in it because his promised word is worth more than any contract, no matter how complete and legal the latter may be. Similarly, in Jesus Christ God uttered the Word that entailed a total commitment on God's part. The sacraments seek to concretize what that means in the various situations of human life. The rites with which we surround the vital and crucial points of our lives are not mere instruments of grace. They are already visible grace, signifying the eruption and explosion of God's saving action in history. When we celebrate the sacraments, we savor by way of anticipation the definitive triumph of God over all human wickedness. Thanks to the sacraments.

12

Sacramental Encounter as Response and Celebration

The Savoldi and Rothaus families were famous in the small city. Hardworking and honest, they were people of strong and violent character. For years, however, a feud had been going on between them. Two members of each family had already been murdered; close relatives had been touched. It seemed to be almost a rerun of the story of Romeo and Juliet and their families. It all began with the breakup of a marriage between members of the two families. They hurled accusations at each other and spread malicious rumors. The atmosphere of hatred grew until crimes were committed.

The parish priest managed to get the Savoldi family to consider a reconciliation. The whole process was helped by a daughter who was a nun and a son who was a seminarian. A true spirit of forgiveness came into being. Several efforts were then made with the Rothaus family, but in vain. The peace overtures met with renewed threats. Reconciliation did not occur or even seem remotely possible, despite the good will of the Savoldi family. It takes two to pick a fight, and two to effect reconciliation. The sun does not help if the plant has withered. Water is no help if the soil is rocky. There is no use in talking if the other party does not want to listen. But if the plant were vigorous, the sun would make it even greener. If the ground were fertile, water would help the seeds to sprout. And if someone were to welcome the message of the other party, that could lead to encounter, then friendship, then love, and then everything that is great on earth.

If we consider the matter closely, we realize that no being lives alone and solitary. Not even the rocks do that. They are embedded in the bosom of the earth, whipped by howling winds, or washed by the waves of the sea. Everything lives in encounter. The whole reality of creation grows and flourishes in the encounter of heaven and earth, male and female, human being and God. It can be no different in the case of the sacraments.

One day Capuchin missionaries came to the city. There were intense prayer services for more than two weeks. They were told about the feud between the Savoldi and Rothaus families. One missionary worked hard and managed to persuade the two families. The sacrament of reconcilition took place. Arms opened wide and the two sides united in friendship and family relatedness. Wine gladdened the hearts of all and made it easier for them to forget old injuries. To this day reports from the city inform me that peace and harmony reign on the smiling faces of the Savoldis and the Rothauses.

Divine Proposal and Human Response

The theology of *ex opere operato* seeks to affirm God's ever present proposal, which never suffers defeat from human rejection. It perdures as a permanent and definitive offer to human beings. But a sacrament is not constituted solely by God's initiative. It is also the human being's response to God's proposal. It is only in and through the humble welcome of the faithful that the sacrament becomes fully real and fruitful in the human soil that is steeped in divine grace. A sacrament basically emerges as a meeting between God, who descends to the human being, and the human being, who ascends to God. Without that meeting, a sacrament remains an incomplete work.

It does not suffice, then, to point up the *ex opere operato* aspect. It is also important to stress the necessity of openness on the part of the human being, the fact that the human being must not put obstacles in the way (*non ponentibus obicem*, as the Council of Trent put it). Trent vigorously reaffirmed the two aspects: the unassailable certainty of God's sympathy, which is never denied even in the face of human rejection; and the urgent need for conversion and the removal of all obstacles so that the encounter between God and the human being may take place and the sacrament become a reality in the fullest sense. The Council of Trent taught that the grace of a sacrament is conferred on the person who does not put obstacles or impediments in the way (DS 1606). If there are such obstacles, then grace is made visible, the act indicative of the Lord's presence in our midst takes place, but he is not welcomed or accepted. The door is closed to him and the drama of the nativity is repeated: he came to his own but his own did not accept him . . . because there was no place for him at the inn (see Jn 1:11 and Lk 2:7).

A Long Process of Preparation and Liberation

It is clear, then, that a sacrament is not simply the rite. Its full realization presupposes a whole life that is opening to God, as a flower to light or as a sunflower to the course of the sun. An essential part of a sacrament is the process of undergoing conversion and searching for God. We should not view a sacrament statically, as something confined in time to the moment when the rite is performed. The ceremony is, as it were, the peak of life's mountain. Before it came the ascent; after it comes the descent. This whole process is part of the sacrament. Human beings have been discovering God and divine grace in the significant actions of life. They have been opening up to God, welcoming God's advent and celebrating God's epiphany. Then, in the official ceremony of the community of faith, they celebrate and savor the divine diaphany in and through the frail fringes of material elements and sacred words. After the sacramental ceremony they will live on the strength imbibed there and prolong the sacrament in and through their lives. Grace will accompany them under other signs, leading them from search to search and from encounter to encounter until they finally reach a final and definitive embrace.

Without conversion, the celebration of a sacrament is an offense against God. It means casting pearls before swine, choosing to perform the acts embodying Christ's maximum visibility in the world without adequate interior purification. One must have one's heart in one's hand for encounter, be pure for love, and be reconciled for feasting. Without proper preparation, encounter is mere formalism, love no more than passion, and banquet no more than orgy.

If individuals receive communion, there ought to be elements of communion in the group in which they live. If they celebrate the sacrifice of Christ and his violent death, they should be ready to undergo the same sacrifice and to live their Christian faith in the same manner. This includes persecution, arrest, and violent death as normal things. If they administer or receive baptism, they should be witnesses to the faith in their community. If they seek reconciliation and find pardon in the sacrament of penance, they should be signs of reconciliation amid the conflicts of society. How could they, in all sincerity of heart, seek and find reconciliation privately in the sacrament, if in their outside lives, their work, and their business affairs they continue to exploit their fellow human beings, to pay unjust wages, and to treat human beings as negotiable commodities. Sacramental reconciliation is insipid if it does not entail an obligation to change one's life; it offends God rather than glorifying God. Paul could rightly warn the Corinthians: without conversion a sacrament is a curse, without preparation it is condemnation (see 1 Cor 11:27-29).

If, on the other hand, people have prepared for a sacrament day by day, then the celebration of it is the vigorous expression of a life illuminated by faith; and it will communicate the Life that vivifies faith and life.

A sacrament, therefore, entails commitment. Indeed, to the early Latin-speaking Christians the word *sacramentum* meant precisely involvement and sacred commitment. It meant commitment to change one's praxis. Conversion was not simply the adoption of new convictions about God, human destiny, and the hope for human liberation through Jesus Christ. Conversion was commitment, first and foremost, involving new attitudes that set Christians against the social setup of the time. It made them subversives, people who were undermining the worship of emperors as gods, the religious values of paganism, and the prevailing ethics of family life. In the early church the sacrament of baptism (the rite) was administered only to those who pledged their commitment *(sacramentum)* to martyrdom. The word *sacramentum* expressed that attitude of commitment. Later the word began to be used for the rite that expressed the attitude: for example, the rite of baptism, the rite of matrimony, the rite of the eucharist, and so forth.

It should now be quite clear that a sacrament signifies the culmination of a whole process of conversion and commitment to the revivifying and liberating cause of Christ. Without the commitment it presupposes, incarnates, and expresses, the rite is magic and mendacity before God and human beings.

13

Two Movements in the Sacramental Universe

A man appeared in Galilee and proclaimed the following. This world has an eternal meaning. Our lives are destined for Life, not for death. The happiness we await from God is a happiness for those who are in tears, for those who are slandered, persecuted, and tortured. We have God's guarantee that this world is destined to have a happy end.

In Galilee this man announced he had good news and great joy for the whole Jewish people. He was the incarnate Son of God, Jesus Christ, our Liberator. He did only good: curing people, forgiving their sins, inspiring hope, and resurrecting the dead. He loved everybody.

And yet he was a cause of scandal. As the experienced and holy old man, Simeon, put it: this child will be a cause of scandal, responsible for the salvation or damnation of many in Israel (Lk 2:34). And so it turned out to be. Some saw him as a glutton and a boozer (Mt 11:19). They said he hung around with the wrong sort of people (Mk 2:16). He was viewed as subversive (Lk 23:2), heretical (Jn 8:48), crazy (Mk 3:20), diabolically possessed (Mk 3:22), and blasphemous (Mk 2:7). Other people, however, saw him very differently. To them he was a just and holy person: teacher, liberator, God's envoy, the savior of the world, God present in person. As the early church put it: for some he is a stumbling block to be picked up from the road and tossed out of the way; for others he is the cornerstone on which the whole edifice is built (1 Pt 2:6; Rom 9:33; Lk 20:17; 1 Cor 3:11).

In the activity of Jesus we can see a symbolic impulse or movement. As the original Greek verb *(sym-ballo)* suggests, he brings together, unites, and points toward God. Jesus was understood and accepted by people of upright hearts who were sincerely seeking salvation and waiting for the definitive liberator of human beings from their present situation of decadence and despair. These people discovered who Jesus was and bore witness to their discovery: "You are the Messiah, the Son of the living God" (Mt 16:17). They bore this witness despite Jesus' meager appearance, lowly origin, and frailty. He exulted in their response: "Blessed are those who are not scandalized by me" (Lk 7:23; Mt 11:6).

There were other people, however, who were locked into their truths and traditions, their selfish societal interests and their religious realities. They were comfortable people who were satisfied with their present lives. They expected nothing because they had everything. If they were waiting for anything, it was for a Messiah who would come and put his seal of approval on their existing privileges, traditions, dogmas, and personal convictions. All these people saw Jesus as a diabolic force. As the original Greek verb *(dia-ballo)* suggests, Jesus seemed to cause separation and division, to jeopardize the existing religion and state. And they were right! Jesus raised questions and called for conversion. He would not legitimize the socioreligious status quo. He called upon human beings to establish a new sort of relationship with their fellow human beings and with God. These demands did not sit well with those who wielded religious, social, and juridical power. Accepting Jesus and his message would entail changing their own praxis. They would have to assume great risks. It was much easier, then as now, to isolate and liquidate the reformer than to engage in the task of reform. So Jesus was slandered, persecuted, arrested, tortured, and crucified.

Jesus Christ was the sacrament of God in the world, the sacrament of light. Light shows up the dark corners of a house, revealing what is there. Either people will accept the light and become children of the light, or they will curse it and try to put it out. Light is bothersome. It hurts the eyes. But light cannot be blamed for shining into the darkness and revealing things that people were trying to hide. As is the case with any sign or signal, light can be understood or misunderstood. It is essentially bound to be *sym*bolic for those who understand it, and *dia*bolic for those who do not understand it. This is the intrinsic risk in every sign, and it was true in the case of Jesus Christ, who was the ultimate, definitive sign of God.

The Symbolic Movement

A sacrament possesses a symbolic thrust or movement: uniting, recalling, making present. *First,* a sacrament presupposes faith. Without faith a sacrament says nothing about anything. Remember the case of our sacramental family mug. It signified and symbolized something more than an ordinary aluminum mug only for those who had lived close to it and shared life with it. Well, only for those who have faith do the sacred rites, the sacramental high points of life, become mysterious vehicles of divine grace and its presence. Otherwise they are mere ceremonies: empty, mechanical, and ultimately ridiculous.

Second, a sacrament expresses faith. Faith basically does not reside in adherence to a creed of theoretical truths about God, humanity, the world, and salvation. Faith is a basic attitude, first and foremost. Not reducible to some other attitude that is even more basic and fundamental, faith is an attitude whereby human beings open themselves up to welcoming a transcendent reality that is heralded in the world as the ultimate Meaning of the world. Religions apply the name God or Mystery to this transcendent reality that is detected in the world. A sacrament is the most authentic form of expressing dialogue with God. There are two sides or movements to this expression. In and through a sacrament, human beings express themselves to God. They worship and glorify God as well as asking for life and forgiveness. God, too, engages in self-expression through a sacrament, offering human beings love, forgiveness, and life. If a sacrament is not an expression of faith, then it has degenerated into mere magic or ritualism. It has completely lost its symbolic dimension.

Third, a sacrament nurtures faith as well as presupposing and expressing faith. In expressing themselves, human beings change both themselves and the world. By ex-carnating and objectifying themselves, they elaborate the words and actions that help to nurture their faith and their religion. A religion is the whole set of historical expressions of faith within the possibilities of a given culture. It is a complex of symbols that expresses and nurtures faith in a perduring way. Sacraments are its heart, grace its pulse.

Fourth, a sacrament concretizes the universal church for a specific crucial situation in life: birth, marriage, eating, sickness, and so forth. Hence it makes little sense for people to want to receive a sacrament of the church if they have no real connection or tie to the church. To experience and live the reality of a specific sacrament, which concretizes the universal sacrament of the church, one must adequately live the experience of the universal sacrament (the church). Only then does a sacrament cease to be mere magic and assume its authentic symbolic function.

Finally, a sacrament embodies and displays a threefold symbolic dimension. It *remembers the past,* where the experience of grace and salvation burst into the world; it keeps alive the memory of the cause of all liberation, Jesus Christ and the history of his mystery. A sacrament also *celebrates a presence in the here and now of faith:* that is, grace being made visible in the rite and being communicated to human life. Thirdly, a sacrament *anticipates the future* in the present: that is, eternal life, communion with God, and the shared banquet with all the just.

It is clear, then, that a sacrament of faith calls for ongoing conversion. To undergo conversion is to keep turning to God and Jesus Christ, not just in thought but in active practice. To undergo conversion is to seek out the presence of God and divine grace in all things and in all situations of life; it is to live in accordance with the presence of God and what it demands of us. Those who are faithful in this search will always find the bright star on their journey. The place of encounter becomes sacred, the action sacramental. Our encounter with the divine is celebrated in words and ceremonies. The signs used by us serve to express this encounter. They are the sacraments of life that celebrate the life of the sacraments.

The Diabolic Movement

A sacrament may also possess a diabolic thrust or movement: separating, scandalizing, and leading to deviations. A sacrament can be distorted into mere *sacramentalism*. People celebrate a sacrament, but without undergoing conversion. They employ the signs symbolizing the Lord's presence, but without preparing their hearts. The sacraments are used to express adherence to a faith, but this faith is sheer ideology without any practical consequences. The lower and middle sectors of the middle class frequently seem to exhibit a sacramentalist Christianity of this sort. Theirs is a faith for one hour a week, a faith for Sunday Mass and a few major moments in life: birth, marriage, burial. They attend rites but they do not live a vital faith in their lives. Their concrete lives embody values that are opposed to the faith: for example, the exploitation of human beings and the greedy quest for more and more wealth.

Another diabolic tendency in the sacramental universe is the *infiltration of a capitalistic spirit*. Some people will take every opportunity to receive a sacrament because they want to accumulate divine grace as if it were just another thing that can be collected and piled up. This sort of sacramental consumptionism, which lacks any real understanding of the dialogic structure of the sacraments and the concomitant prerequisites of faith and conversion, has had a disastrous impact on the mentality of popular Catholicism.

Still another example of the diabolic movement in sacramental practice is the *spirit of magic*. People do not understand and live the rite as a cultural expression of their faith, one which Christ assumes and uses to make himself present and to communicate his love and grace *(ex opere operato)*. Instead, people erroneously think that the sacrament works on its own by virtue of some mysterious power inherent in the sacramental elements. Not Christ but the ceremony itself is the operative cause. Here we have a magical way of interpreting and living the sacraments. Respect and awe for the sacred rite does not express respect and awe over the presence of the Lord. It is little more than a fear of not executing the signs correctly, hence calling down a curse rather than a blessing. Repetition of a sacrament, of baptism, for example, is due to a magical sort of belief: baptism cures the illness of a child so the baby will be baptized as often as it takes to overcome the dangerous problem.

The signs that concretize the definitive victory of grace in the world have been entrusted to human beings. In spite of human unworthiness and sinfulness, they do not fail to make visible the unfailing "yes" that God spoke to all human beings in Jesus Christ. An individual can frustrate the efficacy of a sacrament. Taken as a whole, however, the sacraments guarantee the triumph of grace over sin in and for the here and now of history. By the same token, they can be misused, abused, and turned into signs of condemnation because they have been entrusted to human beings.

Like Jesus Christ, the sacraments inevitably share the ambiguity of any and every sign. They should serve the symbolic process of salvation and grace, but they may serve the diabolic process of perversion and condemnation; because they are sacraments.

14

Conclusions

We can sum up our treatment of the sacramental universe and its structure in a series of statements.

1. A sacrament is a way of thinking, first of all. Sacramental thinking views reality not as a thing but as a symbol. The symbol arises from human encounter with the world. In this encounter both the human being and the world are changed; they become fraught with meaning.

2. As a specific way of thinking, sacramental thinking is universal. In other words, all things, not just some things, can be transformed into sacraments.

3. The structure of human life as such is sacramental. The more human beings relate to the things of this world and other human beings, the more the fan of symbolic and sacramental signification opens out for them.

4. Every religion, be it Christian or pagan, has a sacramental structure as well. Religion is born of the encounter of humanity with the deity. This encounter is mediated and celebrated in the world: in a rock, a mountain, a person, and so forth. The medium of encounter becomes sacramental. These objects, persons, and historical events become sacraments for all those people who had an experience of God by coming in contact with them. Faith does not create a sacrament. It creates in human beings the viewpoint that enables them to see the pres-

ence of God in things and history. God is always present in them but human beings do not always take note of that fact. Faith permits them to glimpse God in the world. Then the world, with its things and events, undergoes transfiguration. It is more than just world; it is now a sacrament of God. The Christian sacraments can be understood only by those people who profess the Christian faith. A Christian sacrament does not cease to be a sacrament insofar as other people are concerned, but they do not grasp it as such. To the uninitiate, the sacramental bread seems to be mere bread, sacramental water mere water. To the Christian, however, that bread is more than bread; it is the body of Christ. And sacramental water makes visible to the Christian eye an inner purification. As Vatican II rightly put it in *Sacrosanctum concilium* (n. 59): "The sacraments do not just presuppose faith. By words and things they also nurture, strengthen, and express it. That is why they are called sacraments of faith."

5. For the Judeo-Christian tradition history is the principal place of encounter with God. It is a history of salvation or damnation. The history of salvation that runs from Adam to the last of the elect is considered a sacrament or mystery.

6. The phases of that history are also called sacraments: the beginnings, Israel, the time of the prophets, the time of Christ, the time of the church, and the eternal life of glory.

7. Jesus Christ, the culminating point of salvation history, is called the primordial or fontal sacrament of God *par excellence.*

8. The phases of Christ's history are also considered sacraments: his birth, infancy, public life, passion, and resurrection.

9. As the prolongation of Christ, the church is called the universal sacrament of salvation.

10. The phases of the mystery of the church are also called sacraments: the church of the beginnings, the church of Israel, the church of Christ, the church of glory.

11. If the whole church is a sacrament, then everything in it and all its actions have a sacramental structure. The liturgy is a sacrament. The service of charity is a sacrament. Prophetic proclamation is a sacrament. The concrete lives of Christians are sacraments.

12. Within this sacramental complex of the church, seven sacraments stand out. They symbolize the totality of human life based on seven fundamental axes. At these pivotal points in life, human beings feel directed to a Force that transcends and sustains them. They see God in them and ritualize these major moments of life in a special way.

13. Jesus Christ is the author of the sacraments because he is the efficacy of all sacraments, both Christian and pagan ones. In a stricter sense he is the author of the sacraments because he, in willing the church, willed the sacraments that concretize and spell out the church in life's various situations.

14. The expression *ex opere operato* means that the infallible presence of grace in the world does not depend on the subjective dispositions of either the one who administers a sacrament or the one who receives it. Grace is present in the sacred rite and manifests the datum of faith that in Jesus Christ God said a definitive "Yes" to humanity. God's "Yes" is not jeopardized by human unworthiness. It is victorious in a definitive way.

15. The infallible presence of grace in the church's rite becomes efficacious only if the human being has an open heart and is prepared. The sacrament becomes fully real only in a two-way encounter: God coming to the human being and the human being going to God. The phrase *ex opere operato* must be pondered in connection with the phrase *non ponentibus obicem*.

91

Only then does God's grace show its smile in the life of a human being.

16. In the early Latin-speaking church, the word *sacramentum* originally signified this conversion of the human being to God. It signified precisely the sacred commitment to live in accordance with the demands of the Christian faith, even if it meant martyrdom. Later the word *sacramentum* came to be used for the rite that expressed the Christian commitment to the liberating message of Jesus Christ: the rite of baptism, the rite of the eucharist, the rite of matrimony, and so forth.

17. Every sign can be turned into a countersign. In every sacrament there inevitably is a symbolic movement that unites and evokes God and Jesus Christ. There can also be a diabolic movement that separates and distances people from God and Jesus Christ. Sacramentalism, sacramental consumptionism, and the turn to magic are distortions of the sacraments. They embody the diabolic impulse in the sacramental universe.

18. A sacrament is a sacrament only in the horizon of faith. A faith that means vital encounter with, and acceptance of, God in one's life expresses its encounter with God through objects, gestures, words, persons, and so forth. These expressions are the sacraments. They presuppose, express, and nourish faith. Because faith implies conversion, a sacrament is efficacious and fully realized in the world only when it expresses conversion and leads to ongoing conversion. A sacrament without conversion is condemnation. A sacrament with conversion is salvation.